Coping with
DEPRESSION

IVY M. BLACKBURN, Ph.D., F.B.Ps.S.

Chambers

Published by W & R Chambers Ltd Edinburgh
First published 1987
Reprinted 1990, 1992 (twice)

Illustrated by James Lyons

British Library Cataloguing in Publication Data

Blackburn, Ivy M.
  Coping with depression.—(Coping with. . .).
  1. Depression—Treatment 2. Self-care, Health
  I. Title
  616.85′2706   RC537

  ISBN 0-550-20517-9

Typeset by Outline, Edinburgh
Printed by Mentor Printers Pte Ltd

Contents

Ivy M. Blackburn is Top Grade Clinical Psychologist at the Royal Edinburgh Hospital, Medical Research Council Brain Metabolism Unit.

Dedication

To the sufferers whom I have had the privilege to help through depression and who taught me so much, and to Professor A.T. Beck who inspired my work. Special thanks to Norma Brearley for the careful preparation of the manuscript and to Mr James Lyons for the illustrations.

Ivy M. Blackburn

Introduction

My aim in this book is not to provide a comprehensive account of all the many forms of depression and its possible causes or treatments, but to describe the main aspects of depression, so that you can recognise it for what it is if you or any of your friends or family show signs of this most common of psychological afflictions. Equally, I hope that this book will help you distinguish normal sadness and unhappiness from depression and will give you ideas for tackling depression.

I shall be describing self-help techniques that have helped many of the people I see every day in the clinic. They can show you how to deal with many of the problems associated with depression and how to reverse the condition before it becomes too severe. Of course, your doctor or a specialist can also offer expert help. Many different types of effective treatments are now available, and it is reassuring to be aware that depression can be completely cured, the sufferer being able to return to his or her previous level of functioning.

The emphasis in this book is on helping you to develop skills of your *own* to combat and prevent depression. It will provide clear guidelines about different problems which may arise. Some of these will refer perhaps to experiences which you have had yourself. The experience of depression is very personal and, in a way, unique to each individual, but there are many common features which can be discussed in a book like this one. Many sufferers have asked me anxiously: 'Have you ever seen somebody as bad as me?' and they have derived some comfort in knowing, from discussion and reading, that there are others like them, indeed that we all have these self-defeating thoughts and crippling feelings at times.

I hope that by trying out some of the suggestions and exercises in this book, whether you are depressed or not, you will be able to increase your general enjoyment of life.

1. What is Depression?

We use the word 'depression' in everyday language to describe a mixture of feelings — sadness, frustration, disappointment and perhaps some lethargy. It is therefore confusing to find that doctors, psychiatrists and clinical psychologists use the term in a different way. For them, depression or depressive illness is a condition which needs specific treatment. Because of the confusion of terms, people who have no experience of depression, either personally or as therapists, may be less sympathetic or helpful than is warranted by the seriousness of the condition. They may feel that the depressed person is lazy, selfish or malingering and may exhort him or her by such phrases as 'pull your socks up' or 'snap out of it, it can't be as bad as that'. Yet, in the course of my work, I have heard mothers say: 'I would rather see my children dead than ever suffer this' or other patients say: 'I would rather have anything else, even cancer, than this.' Sufferers are very aware of the lack of empathy and understanding from friends, colleagues and family, and the fear of being taken for a malingerer adds further to their torment. I have often heard comments such as 'If I had broken a leg, people would know, at least, that there was something wrong with me.'

Depressive Illness

Mood

The symptoms and signs which doctors look for are numerous and affect the whole range of human functions, both psychological and physical.

Depression, as the name implies, is considered to be mainly a disorder of mood or affect, hence the term '*affective illness*' is also often used. The sufferer will describe a low mood or a feeling of being down in the dumps which has persisted for over two weeks, often much longer. The low mood is not necessarily the same throughout the day. Some

1

people may describe feeling worse in the morning and relatively better in late afternoon. This is the 'diurnal variation' which often accompanies the more severe types of depression. Sometimes the depressed mood is a reaction to the environment. The mood may lift for a while if something pleasant happens, for example a visit from a friend or a comedy on television. However, some people who are depressed have an unremitting low mood throughout the day. This low mood is described as something quite different from ordinary sadness: 'it's like a black cloud around my head', 'it's a numb sort of feeling', 'it's like having cotton wool in the head'. Because of this special quality of mood change, some sufferers do not use the term 'depressed' at all. For them, this seems different from the everyday mood changes that we all experience, and it is, indeed, very different. Other moods than sadness can also be present; for example, some people feel more irritable or more anxious than usual.

Thinking

There are also changes in the way people who are depressed think about themselves, their world and their future. The competent housewife or successful businessman may see themselves as being useless, inadequate, incapable, even as total failures. They really believe that they lack 'what it takes' and, therefore, their self-esteem and self-confidence are badly affected. They become indecisive and dwell on past errors or misdeeds and may even feel that they have committed serious crimes or unpardonable sins. They see their world in the same negative terms, as causing nothing but pain, as being frustrating and disappointing. They also feel hopeless as they expect all the pain and suffering to continue for ever. Therefore, as they feel unable to make or contemplate any changes, some may even consider suicide as a solution.

Suicide is a very high risk in depressive illness. Sometimes there may only be a wish to be dead, but often serious attempts at suicide can occur. The accompanying thoughts may be: 'I am a nuisance to my family. They would be better off if I were dead' or 'Dying is the only way of ending my misery'. In Britain each year, 16 out of 100 000 men and women commit suicide and there are probably as many as 50 or more attempts for each fatality. These are likely to be conservative figures as it is reasonable to assume that many more attempts do not come to the notice of the medical services. An individual may, for example, deliberately take a small overdose of sleeping pills, wake up the next day uninjured and not seek medical help. Many parasuicides (attempted suicides) are not just cries for help or impulsive gestures, but are serious attempts where the person genuinely wants to die. Although not all suicides or parasuicides are associated with depressive illness, the risk in depression is very high (30 times higher than in the general population) because of the hopeless and helpless attitude present.

Many other distressing experiences may occur: the diligent housewife or worker feels tired and loses all interest in work, usual activities and hobbies; a previously sociable person may cross the street to avoid friends and turns down all social invitations, thus a vicious cycle of increasing social isolation and depression ensues; there may be continuous worrying and physical symptoms associated with worrying, such as palpitations, excessive sweating, butterflies in the stomach, shaking, dry mouth, diarrhoea or constipation. Thinking can become slow and muddled, concentration can be so impaired that reading or even conversation becomes difficult, so that the sufferer may find it difficult to settle down to anything and may think that there is something wrong with his or her brain.

Physical

The physical symptoms are as distressing as the psychological symptoms — sleep is disturbed, the sufferer either finding it difficult to fall asleep or suffering from frequent wakefulness or waking up early in the morning.

Increased sleep can also occur, though more rarely. Appetite is often diminished, with accompanying weight loss, or sometimes the reverse can occur, increased appetite and weight gain. Many sufferers also experience a loss of energy and a partial or total loss of interest in sex.

A young depressed woman expressed her physical complaints thus: 'I feel exhausted all the time. It is a real effort to do anything. Even keeping myself clean is an effort; I have to drag myself about.' A mother of two young children of school age spent most of her time in bed. She said: 'I feel less bad just lying in bed. I can't sleep, I just lie there. I force myself to get out of bed to send the children to school and then I go back to bed. I get up when they get back from school and then I go back to bed straight after supper. I feel so guilty. The house is a hovel and the children only get junk food. I can't even talk to them.' A successful accountant who had been depressed for several months said: 'Everything seems to be happening too quickly. I can't keep up. I wake up exhausted at 4 am and I can't fall asleep again. Everything seems black, pointless and I am afraid to face the day. The first thoughts which come into my mind are about problems at work and that I won't be able to cope. I don't want people to see me like this. I've given up golf, I don't go to the pub with the boys any more and my wife thinks that I don't love her any more. I have nothing to give to anybody. I would be better off dead.'

Severity

Depression is a serious and painful illness but it can occur in different degrees of severity. You may have been depressed or know somebody who is or was depressed and will recognise perhaps only some of the symptoms that I have listed. Doctors use different terms to describe these different degrees of severity of illness and different treatment approaches are usually recommended. These will be discussed in a later chapter (Chapter 3), but I would like to discuss here just two important ways in which depressive illnesses can differ. Sometimes, the illness can be so severe that the depressed person's thinking is no longer in touch with reality. The ideas of guilt or of illness can become firm beliefs and grossly exaggerated, for example 'I am the cause of all the evil in the world' or 'I have no brain any more'. These types of thoughts are described as delusions and can sometimes be accompanied by abnormal perceptions (hallucinations), for example, hearing an accusatory voice, when there is nobody present, saying: 'You are evil; you should be punished.' Sometimes, the sufferer can become so slowed up that he or she cannot move or speak; or the opposite can occur, for example, restlessness, continuous wringing of hands or rubbing a part of the skin till it looks raw. Such severe depression is classified as *'psychotic'*, is much rarer than the less severe form usually called *'neurotic'*, and is best treated by a short admission to hospital.

The other main distinction relies on the history of the illness. Depressive illness can often recur in the same person. If each episode of illness is a depression, the illness is called *unipolar* recurrent depression. Sometimes, however, a person can be depressed during one episode of illness and excessively happy and cheerful during another episode. There may be various changes in behaviour which are distressing to the family; for example, abundant energy, grandiose ideas of personal power or ability, increased talkativeness, decreased need of sleep, careless spending, increased sexual activity and loss of usual social inhibitions. If periods of depression alternate with periods of this so-called 'manic' behaviour, the illness would then be called *bipolar* or manic-depression. These two types of conditions have been found to be different in many ways and often need different types of treatment.

Who Can Become Depressed?

Depression is so common that it is sometimes described as the common cold of psychiatry and most of us will experience *some* depression at *some* time. Some famous historical personalities are said to have suffered from depression: Napoleon, Churchill, Abraham Lincoln, for example. Children and adolescents can become depressed and some say that animals can also become 'depressed'. Remember the story of Greyfriars' Bobby? A statue in a main street in Edinburgh commemorates this small terrier that watched its master's grave from 1858 until its own death 14 years later. Was this desolate and disconsolate dog 'depressed'? It also seems, from the writings of the ancients and from the Old Testament, that depression has been with us for at least as long as records exist. At any given point in time, about 20% of us will have *some* depressive symptoms, not just sadness, regardless of race and country. The incidence is about twice as high in women as in men, but the reasons for this disproportion are uncertain. It may be that women are more likely to report mood disorders than men or the reasons could be biological (due to hormones and childbirth) or social (women's life circumstances may cause depression) (See Chapter 2). The incidence is lower for more severe depressive illness: about two out of every 100 men and four out of every 100 women suffer from a major depressive illness at any one time, the incidence being lower for bipolar illness (manic-depression) where the sex ratio is more equal (about one in 200 adults).

2. What Causes Depression?

Although you may find 'experts' who may explain depression purely in 'biological', that is physical, terms and others who may, with equal certainty, give purely 'psychological' explanations, it is preferable to try to understand the causes of depression as the result of various interacting factors. If we accept that the brain is the organ of the mind, then biological and psychological, or mental, factors can be seen as just different ways of describing the same events. So, biological explanations describe the physical aspects of depression and psychological explanations describe how depression affects us.

What Role Does Biology Play?

Inheritance

There is much research which indicates that people may inherit genes which make them vulnerable to developing depression. This is apparent in family studies, where it is found that blood relatives of people who have suffered a major depression are more likely to develop depression too. The closer the blood relation is, the greater is the vulnerability. For example, identical twins run more risks (about 65% may develop the illness if their twin has suffered a depression) than non-identical twins who are themselves not more vulnerable than ordinary siblings (14% may share the illness); children and parents are more at risk (about 14%) than nephews and nieces, aunts and uncles and so on of an affected relative. However, it is difficult to separate genetic inheritance from what is learned in the family, that is, the effects of the environment. For this, we need studies of the children of depressed parents, in particular identical twins, who are adopted and raised apart in different families. Such studies are only now being carried out.

The mode of inheritance is not fully understood yet, but it is important to remember that what one inherits is only an increased vulnerability to the illness, not the illness itself. Although many people may inherit the vulnerability, a great number of them may never actually suffer a depressive illness. This suggests that other factors besides genetic inheritance may influence the development of a major depressive illness.

Changes in the brain

Several biological changes in the brain have been found to occur either just before the beginning of a severe depressive illness or during the illness. These are changes in the neuroendocrine or hormone system, changes in certain chemical transmitter systems in the brain, and changes in the electrical activity in the brain. However, there is no permanent change in the brain. All the biological signs disappear when the sufferer recovers and he/she is then indistinguishable from a person who has never had a severe depressive illness.

Hormones

The main hormonal change which occurs in depression is in cortisol, a hormone produced by the adrenal glands, which are located just above the kidneys. The pituitary gland, which lies at the base of the brain, controls the rate at which cortisol is produced. The more severe depressions, whether unipolar or bipolar, are characterised by an over-production of cortisol. This increase in cortisol appears not to be due only to the increase in stress which is associated with being depressed or being in hospital. Rather, the excess in cortisol production is thought to be caused by changes in the hypothalamus, the part of the brain which controls the output of the pituitary gland. Other hormones may also be affected, for example, some studies have shown that drugs which stimulate the pituitary to release growth hormone have a diminished effect in certain depressions.

Neurotransmitters

The millions of nerve cells in the brain communicate with each other by specific chemical substances, called neurotransmitters. It is believed that during depression, there is reduced activity of one or more of these neurotransmitter sytems, particularly of noradrenaline and 5-hydroxytryptamine, in areas of the brain which regulate functions which are disturbed in depression, for example, sleep, appetite, sexual drive and perhaps mood. This reduced level of neurotransmitters would cause reduced communication between the nerve cells and account for the typical symptoms of depression. The evidence for this theory is that certain drugs which reduce these neurotransmitters in the brain can lead to depression, for example reserpine which used to be prescribed to lower high blood pressure. Moreover, those antidepressant drugs which are known to be very effective in the treatment of depression increase the availability of these neurotransmitters in the brain.

Electrical activity

The electrical activity in the brain can be recorded by a sensitive, but harmless, method which involves putting electrodes on the scalp. This produces a record of the different electrical wave forms produced by the brain, the electro-encephalogram (EEG). Studies have shown that there are typical changes in the sleep EEG of people who are severely depressed. The EEG of normal healthy adults shows that sleep is divided into specific stages. Deep sleep is characterised by large deep waves on the EEG and occurs at the beginning of the night, within the first two hours of falling asleep. For the normal healthy adult, there are also four or five periods during the night which are called rapid-eye-movement (REM) sleep. During REM sleep, people are likely to have vivid dreams and their eyes move rapidly. Typically, the first REM sleep occurs about 90 minutes after we fall asleep and may last five to ten minutes. REM sleep may recur every 90 minutes or so through the night and tends to last longer as the night goes on.

During depression, REM sleep comes much earlier, about 25 to 60 minutes after falling asleep, and may occur more often through the night. Depressed sufferers often say that they dream more, generally unpleasant dreams; they enjoy less deep sleep and report feeling not rested when they wake up, as if they had not slept at all.

Do the changes in the brain which I have just described cause depression? This is difficult to assert, because they may just be changes that accompany depression. However, they do show that physiological changes do take place in the brain in some people with depressions, particularly those with 'physical' symptoms of depression, for example, sleep and appetite disturbance, marked loss of interest and of pleasure. Remember that the changes are transient — they disappear with recovery.

What Role Does Psychology Play?

As in the case of biological factors, psychological factors cannot cause depression, but they can increase our vulnerability to depression, and they can help to maintain depression.

Reaction to situations

Although each of us responds to an event in our own way, depending on what is important to us, what we have learned and what our aspirations are, a general class of events is frequently found to precede depression. These can be described as 'loss' events, such as loss of somebody we love through bereavement or separation, loss of a job, loss of friendship, loss of promotion, loss of face and loss of support. Sigmund Freud, at the beginning of this century, proposed mourning and grief as a model for the role of loss in depression. Some researchers have found that a cumulation

of 'life events' often precede the onset of depression. These include severe events, for example, financial worries, severe difficulties with spouses, parents or children and physical illness.

Psychological risk factors

It seems that certain experiences in childhood and certain current life situations make us more vulnerable to respond to these severe events with depression. In a research programme among women in an area of London, a group of sociologists found that women who were more likely to become depressed after experiencing the severe 'life events' which I described above had the following 'vulnerability factors': they had lost their mother in childhood before the age of 11; they currently had no close confidante, that is somebody they could easily confide in; they had three or more children under the age of 14 at home; and they had no job outside the house. It seems that, in the case of women at least, these experiences increase the depressive impact of 'loss' events or of severe life difficulties. The loss of one's mother or father in childhood has been particularly stressed in many investigations.

A risk period for depression in women is middle age. This has sometimes been described as the 'empty nest syndrome', as at this stage the children have often left home and the woman's role needs changing and re-adjusting. This, as many women will recognise, is often difficult to achieve, particularly if there is no external support or if the woman's role and self-esteem were completely dependent on looking after the family.

The way we think and act

A number of other psychological factors have been shown to be associated with depression and in the following chapters, I shall be discussing ways of coping with them. These are thinking patterns which overstress the negative; strict and overdemanding attitudes which we may have developed since childhood; not attributing to ourselves the cause for good events but taking the responsibility only for bad events; organising our lives in such a way that we do not allow ourselves enough pleasure or reward, or 'positive reinforcement' as psychologists call it.

While we cannot do very much about the genes which we inherit, there are well tried procedures which we can follow to prevent us from becoming depressed or to cure depression if it occurs. The next chapter will consider what the specialist can do to help a depressed sufferer and all the following chapters will describe self-help techniques which you yourself can apply. The important thing to remember is that depression can be cured.

3. Treatment of Depression

There are many different treatments for depression, ranging from electroconvulsive therapy to antidepressant medication and to psychotherapy. There are often specific indications why your doctor would recommend one treatment rather than the other, but sometimes the treatments are interchangeable or work best in combination.

Antidepressant Medication

There are two main classes of drugs which have an antidepressant effect: the tricyclic antidepressants and the monoamine oxidase inhibitors, MAOIs for short. These

drugs affect the production, storage and release in the brain of the various neurotransmitter substances which are thought to be associated with depression as discussed in the previous chapter.

Tricyclic antidepressants

The tricyclic antidepressants are called thus because they have a three ring chemical structure. The first tricyclic drug to be used as a treatment for depression was imipramine which was discovered in 1957. Since then, many other tricyclics have been developed and are widely used, for example, amitriptyline, nortriptyline and clomipramine. These drugs are administered in gradual increasing dosages until a dose which is generally regarded as effective is reached, usually about 150 mg day.

Are tricyclic antidepressants effective?

Tricyclic antidepressant drugs have been well tested and are known to be effective in helping sufferers get rid of the symptoms of depression. Mood improves, the sleep pattern returns to normal, concentration, appetite, sexual drive and general interest and other symptoms inprove. On the whole, these drugs are more effective for depressions with more pronounced physical symptoms, that is, with disturbances of sleep, appetite, sexual drive and slowness or agitation. Overall, the findings are that about 75% of such depressed sufferers improve with tricyclic medication. The effects begin to appear after about two to three weeks of treatment, if the right dosage of medication is taken, and often there is considerable improvement at the end of 12 weeks. The medication has to be taken on a daily basis to work. It is usually recommended that the medication should continue to be taken for a further three to six months after recovery, to consolidate improvement and prevent further recurrence of the depression.

Side-effects of tricyclics

Tricyclic antidepressants are not addictive, so that sufferers need not fear that they will find it difficult to stop taking the medication, even if it has been taken for a long period of time. There are mild unpleasant side-effects: mild sedation or sleepiness and dry mouth are common, but tend to wear off after some time. A small percentage of people who take tricyclics complain of some blurring of vision, constipation and trembling. Your doctors will adjust the dosage of medication if such troublesome side-effects occur, or he/she will prescribe a different antidepressant. A sufferer who is taking a tricyclic may continue his or her normal diet, drink alcohol moderately, work and, in fact, continue all his normal activities.

Monoamine oxidase inhibitors (MAOIs)

These make up the second main group of antidepressant medication. Monoamine oxidase, MAO, is an enzyme found in certain tissues of the body, including the brain. It helps to break down neurotransmitters such as noradrenaline and 5-hydroxytryptamine involved in the regulation of emotion and of other functions which are affected in depression. MAOIs inhibit or slow down this process, thus increasing the availability of neurotransmitters in the brain. Two examples of this class of drugs are phenelzine and tranylcypromine. They are now prescribed less commonly than tricyclic medication.

Are MAOIs effective?

Specific kinds of depression have been found to respond best to MAOIs, especially when there is a lot of anxiety and tension present. Sometimes sufferers who have not benefited from tricyclic antidepressant treatment improve with an MAOI. Like tricyclic antidepressant drugs, MAOIs have to be taken daily over several weeks. The time course for improvement is the same as for tricyclics.

Side-effects of MAOIs

MAOIs are also not addictive or habit-forming. Unlike tricyclic medication, MAOIs must not be taken in conjunction with certain medicines and with certain foods which are rich in a chemical called tyramine. Foods which contain high levels of tyramine are certain cheeses, wines, marmite, well hung game and pickled herring. These are given as examples and there are many more such foods. If your doctor prescribes an MAOI for you, he or she will give you a full list of foods and medications you must avoid. Tyramine-rich foods taken in combination with an MAOI can raise blood pressure dangerously.

Newer antidepressant medications

There are a number of newer antidepressant medications, which are neither tricyclics nor MAOIs, which are as effective, and may have fewer side-effects. Examples of these are mianserin and trazadone.

Lithium

Lithium is a completely different type of medication from the two main classes of antidepressants described above. It is not normally used for the treatment of a current depression, but helps prevent depressive relapses. It is, in fact, the lightest known metallic element and we all have it in our bloodstream in small amounts. Although the effect of lithium has been known since the 1940s, it came into use only in the late 1960s. Lithium is also taken daily and the dose is increased gradually until a concentration of lithium in the bloodstream is registered within ranges which are considered necessary for the medication to work. The lithium level in the blood is then monitored regularly while the treatment with lithium continues. Lithium is sometimes combined with other antidepressant medications to increase the effect in some severe depressions.

Is lithium effective?

Although it is not precisely known how lithium works, it has been shown to be very effective, particularly in bipolar illness, that is manic-depression (see Chapter 1). Some sufferers have frequent recurrences of depression and/or mania, when they have started taking lithium continuously, many have had no more, or significantly fewer episodes of illness. Overall, when large numbers of sufferers are followed up, the rate of recurrence of illness is found to be markedly reduced.

Side-effects of lithium

As with tricyclics and the MAOIs, lithium is neither addictive nor habit-forming, but there may be some unpleasant side-effects. Just after starting lithium, there may be slight sleepiness, increased irritability and shakiness or trembling. These effects tend to wear off after a while. Some people may put on weight while taking lithium. If the concentration of lithium in the bloodstream becomes too high, there are many toxic effects: nausea, vomiting and diarrhoea; slurred speech, staggering, mental confusion and irregular heart beat. However, your doctor ensures that these toxic effects do not occur, by taking blood samples at regular intervals to monitor the blood level of lithium. Also, because of the long experience with prescribing lithium, safe dosages of this drug are well known to doctors.

Electroconvulsive Therapy (ECT)

ECT was first introduced as a treatment for mental illness during the 1930s. Although it has received a poor press over the last 10 to 15 years, it has been shown to be extremely effective for certain types of depression. In this country, ECT is only given for very severe depressions when the sufferer has delusions (as described in Chapter 1) and/or is severely slowed down or agitated, has lost a lot of weight, has marked insomnia, especially waking early in the morning, and invariable low mood which does not react to happy situations. It is also sometimes used when there has been no response to antidepressant medication or if medication is contraindicated because of a concurrent physical illness, for example a serious heart condition.

ECT is safe, painless and has remarkably few side-effects. First, the sufferer is given an anaesthetic to induce sleep and then an injection is given to relax the muscles. Once he or she is asleep and prevented from moving, an electric current is applied to the head by means of electrodes (small metal plates) which are applied to the temple. The electric current lasts for a very short while, about 0.1 to 0.5 seconds, and induces what is called a seizure or a fit. There are no limb movements during the seizure, because of the muscle-relaxant and because the sufferer is immobilised. The seizure is over in about a minute, then the muscle relaxant and the anaesthetic wear off and the person wakes up.

This treatment is usually reserved for in-patients. ECT is usually given once or twice a week and normally about five to ten treatments are necessary for the treatment of severe depression.

How does ECT work and are there side-effects?

As for many medical treatments which work, it is not clearly understood why ECT has an antidepressant effect. It is known, however, that a convulsion or seizure is essential for it to work.

The positive side is that ECT can work very quickly and it has fewer bad effects on the heart than many antidepressant medications. On the negative side, ECT causes some temporary memory impairment, which does not last for more than a week or two. Depression itself is known to impair memory function, so that the effect of ECT on memory can be confused with the impairment due to the depression itself. Secondly, immediately after treatment, there can be a brief period of confusion which can last up to one hour. The person who has just had ECT may not know where he or she is and may not be able to comprehend what is happening around him or her. However, this confusion clears away completely after a while and is due solely to the seizure induced by the electrical current.

Some of the criticisms directed at ECT have probably been warranted in the past when ECT was given too indiscriminately, without adequate precautions such as the use of a muscle relaxant and without careful explanation to the sufferer. Nowadays, ECT is never given without the signed consent of the sufferer or of a close relative, it is administered in a safe manner and all possible care is taken to prepare the sufferer in a humane fashion. In fact, very few people are now treated with ECT as it is often a second choice treatment, when there has been no response to antidepressant medications and/or psychotherapy.

The beneficial therapeutic effect of ECT on some sufferers can be very dramatic. Some sufferers and their relatives who have experienced the success of ECT often demand ECT treatment if there is a recurrence of illness, because they want to end the suffering quickly and safely.

Psychotherapy

Psychotherapy is a treatment method used by psychiatrists and psychologists to help sufferers with various psychological problems. It involves talking about your problems with a psychotherapist either in a one-to-one situation (individual psychotherapy) or in a small group with one or two psychotherapists (group psychotherapy).

There are many types of psychotherapy which derive from different theoretical understandings, some commonly used by many professionals, but others fairly unusual and untried. Some psychotherapies can help depression, but some might even make it worse. Psychotherapy can work on its own, as medication can work on its own, and sometimes combining psychotherapy with medication can be more useful for some individuals.

It is impossible to describe all the different approaches to psychotherapy in this book, but two main types of psychotherapy can be distinguished, psychodynamic psychotherapy on the one hand and cognitive and behavioural psychotherapy, on the other.

Psychodynamic psychotherapy

This type of therapy was first developed by Sigmund Freud in Vienna at the beginning of this century. In its classic form, known as psychoanalysis, it is a long-term therapy, lasting several years, which is given individually. It is called psychodynamic therapy because it looks for the cause of people's disturbance in internal conflicts and motivations which derive from childhood experiences. For example, Freud understood depression as anger turned inwards, instead of being expressed towards some close person with whom the sufferer has got a love-hate or ambivalent relationship. The concept of ambivalence is central to the psychoanalytic understanding of depression, involving conflicts between opposing emotions. It is thought to derive from disappointments and frustrations in childhood which exert a lasting influence on the depressed person's life. Psychoanalytic psychotherapy, therefore, involves prolonged treatment to work through the deep conflicts which originate from childhood experiences and to bring about important personality changes.

As classical psychoanalysis is, by definition, long-term, it has not been useful in the treatment of severe, acute depression. More recently, short-term psychodynamic psychotherapies have been developed and are used in the treatment of depression. There have not been large-scale studies to test how effective these short-term psychotherapies are relative to other methods of treatment, but there have been several reports of individual cases. These reports have shown that short-term psychodynamic therapy is successful in the treatment of depression.

However, as this book is going to focus mainly on self-help methods, which you can learn and apply yourself, I shall not go into more details about this type of therapy. To use psychodynamic methods to deal with depression, the sufferer needs to see a therapist who specialises in these techniques.

Cognitive and behaviour therapies

Both cognitive and behaviour therapy are short-term therapies which differ from psychodynamic therapy in that they deal with the here and now and not with childhood conflicts. They both assume that behaviours which are not helpful have been learnt and can be unlearnt. Typically, behavioural or cognitive treatment of depression would last about three months and take 15 to 20 sessions of one hour with a therapist. Both can be given in individual or group format. Behaviour therapy assumes that depression results primarily from a lack or loss of reward in a person's life and, therefore, a lot of emphasis is put on increasing the level of satisfaction a person receives through pleasant activities, relaxation and assertive behaviour. Cognitive therapy is a more recent approach, developed specifically for the treatment of depression. It puts more emphasis on the thoughts and attitudes which maintain depression. Consequently, a number of techniques are used to get at and change these thoughts and attitudes. These techniques involve ways of working directly on thoughts but they also include working on behaviour, for example, pleasant activities, relaxation and assertive behaviour, with the view of changing the way a person thinks about himself, his world and his future.

The rest of this book is going to show you how you can learn cognitive and behavioural techniques to deal with depression. Although you may need to see a specialist to receive cognitive-behavioural treatment, many of the techniques are easily learned and you can apply them yourself — as you will see if you read on.

Supportive therapy

In addition to psychotherapy there are also more general 'talking therapies' sometimes described as counselling or supportive therapy or non-directive therapy which you can receive from your general practitioner or some other professional such as a psychiatrist or psychologist, a social worker or a nurse therapist. These types of therapies differ from psychodynamic and cognitive-behavioural therapies, in that they have not evolved from a theoretical background which aims to explain why people may become depressed. They can nonetheless be helpful if the therapist has the qualities which have been shown to be essential for any therapy to work — these are warmth, genuineness and understanding. The supportive therapist can help by giving you a chance to air your problems, by offering advice and reassurance and by being willing to listen to and understand your personal concerns.

4. How to Measure Depression

It would be useful for you to be able to judge how depressed you are and to measure how well you are doing as you practise the various coping techniques which you will read about in this book. I shall describe two simple ways in which you can do that.

You can use a scale of your own from say 0 to 100. Think of 0 as not depressed, the best that you yourself have ever felt. Try to recall an occasion in your life when you felt really good. All right, have you got it? Call that 0. Now think of an occasion or a period in your life when you felt in your lowest mood, when you felt right down in the dumps. Have you remembered such an occasion? Call that 100. Now you have your own personalised scale and you can place yourself anywhere on that scale according to how you feel at this precise moment or you can try to strike an average for the day as a whole.

A variant on this method of rating mood is to draw a line of 100 millimetres. Call one end 'not at all depressed' and the other end as 'very depressed'. You can put a cross anywhere on the line to measure your mood.

Rating your mood in this way will help you become sensitive to small mood changes, so that you can take preventive steps if you find your mood going down. You will read in this book about different methods to help improve mood — these include distraction, engaging in pleasant activities, increasing your activity level, correcting negative bias in your thinking and challenging your rigid attitudes which get you into no-win situations.

Another advantage of using your own personalised rating scale, is that it stops you from catastrophising situations. Instead of thinking: 'I feel dreadful' or 'I feel terrible', you may find that relative to the worst that you have been (100), you may rate only 40 or 52 or 63. This would help to put your feelings in perspective.

The other method to rate depression in general, rather than just depressed mood, is to use a self-rating scale which is used by researchers and clinicians in conjunction with ratings which they make themselves. A self-rating scale means that you rate yourself on several items which describe symptoms of depression. There are several such scales, but the Beck Depression Inventory (BDI), listed below, is possibly the most widely used one. The BDI is a multiple choice questionnaire. Circle the number next to the answer that reflects best how you have been feeling in the *last week*. If you cannot decide between two answers, circle the higher number.

Beck Depression Inventory

1. 0 I do not feel sad.
   1 I feel sad.
   2 I am sad all the time and I can't snap out of it.
   3 I am so sad or unhappy that I can't stand it.

2. 0 I am not particularly discouraged about the future.
   1 I feel discouraged about the future.
   2 I feel I have nothing to look foward to.
   3 I feel that the future is hopeless and that things cannot improve.

3. 0 I do not feel like a failure.
   1 I feel I have failed more than the average person.
   2 As I look back on my life, all I can see is a lot of failure.
   3 I feel I am a complete failure as a person.

4. 0 I get as much satisfaction out of things as I used to.
   1 I don't enjoy things the way I used to.
   2 I don't get real satisfaction out of anything any more.
   3 I am dissatisfied or bored with everything.

5. 0 I don't feel particularly guilty.
   1 I feel guilty a good part of the time.
   2 I feel quite guilty most of the time.
   3 I feel guilty all of the time.

6. 0 I don't feel I am being punished.
   1 I feel I may be punished.
   2 I expect to be punished.
   3 I feel I am being punished.

7. 0 I don't feel disappointed in myself.
   1 I am disappointed in myself.
   2 I am disgusted with myself.
   3 I hate myself.

8. 0 I don't feel I am any worse than anybody else.
   1 I am critical of myself for my weaknesses or mistakes.
   2 I blame myself all the time for my faults.
   3 I blame myself for everything bad that happens.

9. 0 I don't have any thoughts of killing myself.
   1 I have thoughts of killing myself, but I would not carry them out.
   2 I would like to kill myself.
   3 I would kill myself if I had the chance.

10. 0 I don't cry any more than usual.
    1 I cry more now than I used to.
    2 I cry all the time now.
    3 I used to be able to cry, but now I can't cry even though I want to.

11. 0 I am no more irritated now than I ever am.
    1 I get annoyed or irritated more easily than I used to.
    2 I feel irritated all the time now.
    3 I don't get irritated at all by the things that used to irritate me.

12. 0 I have not lost interest in other people.
    1 I am less interested in other people than I used to be.
    2 I have lost most of my interest in other people.
    3 I have lost all of my interest in other people.

13. 0 I make decisions about as well as I ever could.
    1 I put off making decisions more than I used to.
    2 I have greater difficulty in making decisions than I used to.
    3 I can't make decisions at all any more.

14. 0 I don't feel I look any worse than I used to.
    1 I am worried that I am looking old or unattractive.
    2 I feel that there are permanent changes in my appearance that make me look unattractive.
    3 I believe that I look ugly.

15. 0 I can work about as well as before.
    1 It takes an extra effort to get started at doing something.
    2 I have to push myself very hard to do anything.
    3 I can't do any work at all.

16. 0 I can sleep as well as usual.
    1 I don't sleep as well as I used to.
    2 I wake up 1-2 hours earlier than usual and find it hard to get back to sleep.
    3 I wake up several hours earlier than I used to and cannot go back to sleep.

17. 0 I don't get more tired than usual.
    1 I get tired more easily than I used to.
    2 I get tired from doing almost anything.
    3 I am too tired to do anything.

18. 0 My appetite is no worse than usual.
    1 My appetite is not as good as it used to be.
    2 My appetite is much worse now.
    3 I have no appetite at all any more.

19. 0 I haven't lost much weight, if any, lately.
    1 I have lost more than 5 pounds.
    2 I have lost more than 10 pounds.
    3 I have lost more than 15 pounds.
    I am purposely trying to lose weight by eating less Yes.... No....

20. 0 I am no more worried about my health than usual.
    1 I am worried about physical problems such as aches and pains, or upset stomach, or constipations.
    2 I am very worried about physical problems and it is hard to think of much else.
    3 I am so worried about my physical problems, that I cannot think about anything else.

21. 0 I have not noticed any recent change in my interest in sex.
    1 I am less interested in sex than I used to be.
    2 I am much less interested in sex now.
    3 I have lost interest in sex completely.

This Inventory lists all the symptoms of depression, which you read about in Chapter 1. Add up the score you obtained in each section. A guide to assess how depressed you are and how well you are doing in treatment is: 0-9, no depression; 10-14, borderline depression; 15-20, mild depression; 21-30, moderate depression; 31-40, severe depression; 41-63, very severe depression.

If you score 15 and over, it may be advisable to consult your doctor, especially if you score on items 2, 9, 16, 17, 18 and 19. However, low mood affects all of us from time to time. You may find that you score 15 or over one week, but that this state does not last. You may feel much better after a few days. Real depression lasts for at least two weeks.

You will notice that the self-help techniques described in this book deal with many of the difficulties and symptoms listed in this inventory. Your scores on the different items will help you decide which techniques to apply. However, remember these techniques aim to help you *cope* with depression, but not treat severe depression. You may need expert help as well. If you are reluctant to seek help, although you know that you need it, why not write down your negative thoughts relating to seeking help and answer them in the ways you will learn to do in this book.

5. A New Treatment for Depression

As you read the previous chapters, you will have become aware of how extensive the effects of depression can be. Has this made you feel gloomy? Before you become even more depressed, let me tell you about new methods of coping with mood disorders which psychological research has shown to be effective. You will be able to learn these simple methods to overcome the various ways in which depression can affect you. First, it is important to remember that depression is an illness, not a permanent personality change, and you can learn to combat it.

Cognitive Therapy

In the last decade, a group of psychiatrists and psychologists have developed and tested a new approach to the understanding of depression which has led to new techniques of treatment. The original work was done at the University of Pennsylvania School of Medicine by Professor A.T. Beck and his group, and since then many other clinicians, including some British research groups, have conducted careful studies of the success of these techniques. This new approach is called *cognitive therapy*. It has been shown to be more effective than other types of psychotherapy and as effective, if not more effective, than standard drug treatment for depression. There is also evidence that cognitive therapy reduces the risk of the recurrence of depression. What is *cognitive therapy?* The basic principle is simply that your mood reflects the way you think or, put another way, you create your moods by your 'cognitions' or thoughts. Cognitions refer to the way you look at things, all your interpretations, perceptions, reflections, mental images, beliefs and attitudes. Let me give you some examples.

I wondered at the beginning of this chapter whether you might have felt somewhat gloomy reading about depression. If this is so, try and check on what you have been thinking.

Could it be something like 'Depression is a terrible illness and it is so common. I could not cope with that' or maybe 'This is going to be another one of those books. It's going to make me feel worse'. On the other hand, you could be feeling interested and hopeful and in this case, your thoughts would be quite different. You might be saying to yourself, 'This may be interesting. I'd like to see whether there are ways in which I can help my mood.' Thus different expectations and different interpretations may lead to quite different feelings.

The connection between thoughts and feelings has been known for a long time; for example, a philosopher of the third century BC wrote 'Men are disturbed not by things but by the view they take of them'. You can check this out from your experience. If you *think* 'my friends really like and appreciate me' you feel good, a nice warm glow comes over you. On the other hand, if you think 'they do not really care, they are just putting up with me out of pity,' you feel lousy. Thus, though cognitive therapy differs from the traditional view of depression as an emotional disorder, it pays a lot of attention to feelings because they are the clue to thoughts. Cognitive therapy offers methods for relieving distressful feelings through the cognitions or thoughts which sustain them. If you are depressed, all your thinking relating to yourself, your situation and your future becomes increasingly more negative and what is more you believe that these interpretations are actually true. You believe that things are really as bad as you imagine them. However, in clinical practice and in research, we have found that negative interpretations and attitudes nearly always contain gross distortions and errors, although they may appear plausible and valid to the depressed person. The therapy helps you to stand back from your interpretations and examine and correct them objectively using your own reasoning ability. This book will help you develop problem-solving and coping techniques to deal not only with minor mood changes but also with more important emotional problems and life problems.

Unlike traditional psychotherapy, cognitive therapy is short-term and brings rapid improvements, often in as short

a time as three months. You work in collaboration with your therapist, gaining understanding of the relation between events, thoughts and feelings, learning to distinguish appropriate from inappropriate feelings, reasonable from unreasonable interpretations and attitudes. You also learn how to combat symptoms like inactivity, tiredness and social inadequacy through simple self-control techniques. Once you've learned these self-control techniques, you can apply them in the future whenever you begin to get depressed and thus prevent a recurrence of illness.

Does cognitive therapy work?

In case this appears too good to be true, I would like to give you some examples of the studies which have been conducted, as I am sure that you would like to know whether there is any evidence for what I say. A group of psychiatrists and psychologists from the University of Pennsylvania, in Philadelphia, compared the success of cognitive therapy with a standard antidepressant medication (imipramine) in

41 depressed individuals attending an out-patient clinic. They found that at the end of 12 weeks there was considerable improvement in both groups, but the group who received cognitive therapy showed more improvement and more of them remained in treatment. At the end of one year the superiority of cognitive therapy remained. It was important that other researchers who had not been involved in the development of cognitive therapy and who, therefore, might be more objective, test out these promising results. Several other centres have conducted careful treatment trials and found substantially the same results. We have done so in Edinburgh, in both hospital out-patient clinics and in general practice surgeries, and found that cognitive therapy was an effective method of treatment. More importantly, two years after treatment, there was far less recurrence of depression in the groups who had received cognitive therapy. Research continues but we are most encouraged by our findings so far. We find that severely depressed sufferers who attend hospital clinics may sometimes need up to 16 weeks treatment and that for them adding antidepressant medication may give a better result than either treatment on its own, but for many others the psychological approach alone is most effective.

This book is a practical application designed to help you cope with and combat depression, using the well tried techniques used in cognitive therapy. There will be a number of examples to help you learn and apply the techniques. You can try and use them by yourself whether you are depressed or have just recovered or are still recovering from depression. You may also find that the techniques increase your well-being, even if you have never been depressed and you may apply them as a preventive measure.

If you are too depressed to apply the techniques on your own, ask your general practitioner to refer you to a professional cognitive therapist. Most health services now have clinical psychologists or psychiatrists who are trained cognitive therapists and they will be able to help you apply the techniques while you use the book as a back-up.

6. How Thinking is Linked with Depressed Feelings

You and I tend to believe implicitly what we think and to consider that thoughts are a true reflection of reality. The first thing to remember is that thoughts are just interpretations of reality. When we are depressed our interpretations can be very biased and the bias is always negative. I have noticed that whatever people's status or intelligence, when they are depressed they tend to make the same sorts of errors when they think about themselves, their own circumstances or their future. The list that follows shows the errors that you must look out for.

1. Overgeneralising

You think that because an unpleasant thing happened to you once, it will *always* happen and therefore you feel upset. A young man who felt lonely, unwanted and rejected thought that he would *never* be able to have a girlfriend as girls did not find him attractive. He had asked a girl from the office out and she turned him down. This meant that all other girls he invited out would do the same thing. A young mother who had upset her child by one of her comments said: 'I can never say the right thing'. A middle-aged man assured me that nothing ever went right for him. 'If I make travel arrangements, something always goes wrong; if there are birds in the square and tens of people about, you can be sure that it will be me the birds foul on; when I am in a hurry all the lights turn red; if I buy a new car somebody always crashes into me'.

A senior university lecturer who received an impatient comment from a bus conductor because he did not have the right change thought: 'everybody treats me as dirt'. When you label yourself as 'a loser' or 'stupid' or 'totally hopeless'

you are using the extreme terms of overgeneralisation, that is you give yourself a general label on the basis of perhaps one mistake or one failure.

2. Personalising

You think that you are solely responsible for a negative or unpleasant event, when often there is little basis for this conclusion in fact. A mother of two thinks that her children are quarrelling about which programme to watch on television because she is so inadequate. A passer-by frowns and you think 'he finds me disgusting'. People do not appear to be enjoying themselves very much at a party and you think: 'it is my fault, I am not entertaining enough'. Personalising gives you an unrealistic sense of responsibility and therefore makes you unnecessarily guilty. You carry the weight for everything that goes wrong; everything is related to some deficiency or inadequacy in yourself. You overlook the part that others may have played and you are confusing the possibility that you may have contributed to what has happened with the possibility that it is all your fault.

3. Black and white thinking

This refers to the tendency to evaluate yourself, other people and situations in extreme categories. Watch out for the either/or reasoning. Either you succeed at everything or you are a failure; either you work hard at all times or you are lazy; either you're a good mother at all times or you're a bad mother. Black and white thinking always goes the same way. You usually see others as white and you as black. Other people are happy and you are not; other people cope and you can't; other people are successful and you are not. Black and white thinking does not allow for degrees of anything: 'I am a total failure', 'I am totally stupid', 'I am totally unattractive'. This way of thinking is unrealistic because people or situations are rarely totally one thing or another. It also leads to perfectionism and the likelihood of never quite meeting the stringent demands that you make upon yourself, thus getting caught in the 'no win' situation.

4. *Jumping to conclusions*

You jump to a negative conclusion when there is insufficient evidence to do so, even when there is no evidence at all.

A young woman took her baby to her doctor's surgery for inoculation. She came back and said to me 'All the other mums there were looking down on me. They thought I was a bad mother'. She was not able to give any evidence to support this conclusion, except that she was the youngest mother in the waiting room. This is an example of mind-reading, when she was so convinced that her assumption was correct that she did not bother to query it. Suppose your friend does not telephone you back and you conclude 'He or she finds me boring', only to discover later that your message was not passed on. Jumping to negative conclusions would have made you feel bad unnecessarily. You arrange to meet some people at a certain time and they are late so that you have to wait 15 minutes. You feel sad as you say to yourself: 'they don't care for me, they don't think very much of me'. When they finally arrive you are very quiet and restrained and do not take part in the conversation. There could well be different, less depressing reasons why they were late, but your behaviour might perhaps provoke a negative reaction from your friends and thus appear to validate your conclusion.

Sometimes you can jump to unrealistic negative conclusions about the future, as if you had a crystal ball in which you see only misfortunes. Depressed clients often tell me 'I know I won't get better. This is going to go on and on'. Others predict that they will lose all their friends, that financial disaster is going to strike, that they will lose their job, or that they will never enjoy anything any more. This negatively biased fortune-telling can only increase your depressed feelings and create intense hopelessness regarding the future. It can even make you feel that life is not worth living and stop you from adopting a problem-solving attitude. An accountant who was seeing me for cognitive therapy had created the following scenario in his mind: 'I'm going to lose my job and I shall not be able to support my family or pay my mortgage. The debt collectors will be knocking at the door. I will be put in prison where I will be maltreated'. This man, who is now well and back at work, seriously thought that he would be better off dead as he was convinced that his fortune-telling was correct.

5. *Catastrophising*

You say to yourself: 'I made a dreadful mistake' or 'This is terrible! I will never be able to show my face again' or 'I am ruined'. You are likely to be blowing a mistake or a fault out of proportion while devaluing the positive aspects of your behaviour or of the situation. You are magnifying your faults or liabilities and minimising your qualities. This biased view leads to low self-esteem and lack of confidence in oneself.

Would you agree with the beautiful model who thought she was unpresentable because she had a small spot on her chin or would you condemn out of court a child's careful essay because of the one spelling mistake? Catastrophising is like that — not seeing all the positive aspects because of the minor negative ones.

6. *Disqualifying the positive*

This often takes the form not only of ignoring positive aspects of situations and concentrating on minor negative aspects, but worse, of changing the positive into the negative. See whether you recognise any of these examples: somebody pays you a compliment on your appearance and you think 'They are just saying that, because they think I look really awful'; your boss tells you that you are doing a really good job and you think 'He thinks that I am incompetent and that jollying me on will help'. A young women went back to work after a few weeks of illness and her colleagues enquired after her health and tried to ease her work load. She said to herself 'Because I've been ill, they don't think I can do my job anymore'. A middle-aged executive is promoted to a job in a new office and he thinks 'They want rid of me'. A student who gets one B grade and three A grades in her examinations feels depressed as she says to herself: 'I'm a failure; I'm not bright enough, as I always knew'.

This way of thinking derives from a deep-seated deprecating view of oneself. Disqualifying the positive and abstracting the negative out of every situation help confirm this view and create intense misery.

7. 'Should' statements

You are like a very implacable task-master, with arbitrary and impossible rules both for yourself and others. 'I should have been able to do that', 'I should have known how she felt', 'People should keep their promises', 'He should have arrived on time' are the types of statements which create constant disappointment with oneself, guilt, shame, frustration and anger with others. Such excessively high standards and expectations are not compatible with our all-too-human day-to-day performance and, therefore, imply continual failure and bad feelings.

General characteristics

These examples indicate how depressed and generally unpleasant feelings can be caused by distorted interpretations of what goes on around you. So, stop a moment and check whether at the back of your mind you have a thought like 'Not only do I feel bad, even my thinking is wrong'.

I have heard depressed individuals make this comment when they begin to understand the relationship between feelings and thinking. Well, I would like to make three important points before you go on with the more practical chapters that follow:

1. Your thinking is not wrong, because we are not talking in terms of 'right' and 'wrong' and thoughts are just interpretations. It is just that some of your interpretations are excessively negatively biased or harsh.

2. Not all your thinking is biased in this way, only those thoughts relating to evaluation of yourself, your future and certain aspects of your environment. In other respects, for example, evaluation of others, or solving a mathematical problem or a problem of logic, or evaluation of a film or a book, your thinking does not differ markedly from that of others.

3. Your feelings are inextricably tied up with your thoughts or interpretations. You can change the depressed feelings and your behaviour by learning to correct these negative biases in your thinking. The next chapters will help you learn techniques to do that.

7. How to Defeat Inactivity

You saw in Chapter 1 that tiredness, lethargy, loss of interest, loss of motivation, loss of pleasure and indecisiveness can be symptoms of depression. These can lead to ever-increasing inactivity which, in its turn, causes problems of its own — self-criticism, guilt, criticism from others and perhaps a daunting amount of accumulated things to do. A depressed lawyer told me that he had not answered any letters for three months. Where was he to start? A housewife had not cleaned or done any washing or ironing for four weeks:

> 'There's a mountain of ironing to do. I can't cope. I don't know what to do first'.

Inactivity is self-defeating, because people invariably say that it does not make them feel better. On the other hand, there is a lot of evidence that the more people do and the more pleasant activities they engage in, the better they feel. Then, why don't depressed people do more? Some well-meaning friend or relative may say to them: 'Pull your socks up and get on with it'. This type of exhortation is, actually, most unhelpful because the sufferer is likely to be saying the same thing to himself or herself without success. He or she may, in addition, be saying: 'I'm no good; I'm lazy' or 'I'm inconsiderate'. Making such comments to oneself does not help; it probably makes us feel worse.

The reasons for the inactivity are partly physical, because of the physiological changes which may occur in our body, but also because of the defeating statements which we might be making to ourselves.

Thoughts which Lead to Inactivity

Here are some examples of action-defeating statements we make to ourselves. See whether you recognise them. In the right-hand column are suggestions for ways in which you can challenge these thoughts.

Negative thoughts which stop you from doing things	*Possible answers*
There's too much to do. I can't cope.	I can write down what I need to do. Maybe it won't seem so overwhelming then. I don't have to do everything today. I can take things step by step.
It's too difficult.	It seems difficult because I'm depressed. I've done this many times before.
I've already wasted far too much time. There's no point in doing anything now. It will only make me feel worse.	Not getting on with it does not make me feel better. I can make a start and see how I get on.
I won't enjoy it.	How do I know that? I am fortune-telling again. Try it and see.
I'll wait until I feel better.	If I wait until I feel like it, I may never do it. Doing it now may make me feel better.
What's the point, it won't make me feel better.	At least doing it will stop me worrying about it. How do I know it won't make me feel better? It certainly cannot make me feel worse.

Negative thoughts which stop you from doing things	*Possible answers*
I won't be able to do it as well as I used to.	Maybe so. But it's more likely that I shall give myself a bad mark without good reason, because I'm depressed. The important thing is to do it, not to do it perfectly.
So, I cleaned the kitchen yesterday. So what?	Normally that wouldn't be a big thing at all. But it's extremely difficult at the moment. I did it in spite of that. I can give myself credit for that.

These are some ways in which you can challenge the thoughts that are making you procrastinate and unable to get on with what you want to do. Later on, you will read in more detail how to deal with such negative thoughts.

Practical Ways of Getting Rid of Inactivity

There are also practical things that you can do. Remember that increasing your activity is helpful to break the vicious circle of depression for many reasons. First, it may distract your mind from painful thoughts; secondly, it will give you a sense of control over your own life; thirdly, it may make you feel more worthwhile; fourthly, you may enjoy things once you try them; fifthly, paradoxically, activity may actually make you feel less tired. Normally, when you are tired, you need a rest. But when you are depressed, doing nothing will only make you feel more lethargic and exhausted. Sixthly, increasing your activity level will also increase your motivation; the more you do, the more you'll feel like doing.

Once you get started, problems which appeared insoluble may come into perspective. Finally, people who matter to you will be pleased and this will give you pleasure in turn.

First, it's a good idea to find out exactly what you're doing. I find that sometimes depressed people are doing more and enjoying more things than they give themselves credit for. So, you can keep a record for a few days on an activity schedule which records what you do every hour of the day.

On page 46 is an example of an activity schedule with two days activities filled in.

Once you've got used to filling in a schedule like the one shown below, begin to rate each activity for M (Mastery) on a scale of 0-10 and for P (Pleasure) also on a scale of 0-10. So M-0 would indicate no sense of achievement and M-10 would mean considerable achievement. P-0 would indicate that you have not enjoyed the activity at all and P-10 would mean that you derived great enjoyment or pleasure from it. Remember to rate your activities for M and P as near to the time of the activity as possible; if you wait till later your depression may cause you to devalue or discount what you've done. Remember also when you rate for M that you are rating for how difficult the activity is for you *now* and the corresponding achievement for doing it *now*, not for how difficult it was before you got depressed.

Having done the schedule, you may find that you are doing more than you thought you were or that you are more competent than you imagined you were. This will correct some of your negative thoughts. However, you may have been right. Maybe you were doing as little as you thought. The next step is then to plan each day in advance. Be careful not to schedule too many things at once or activities which are too difficult. It is better to go about building up your activities in a gradual way, starting with simple things. Remember to schedule in pleasant activities, that is, activities which *used to be* pleasurable for you. A plan will help with indecision, for example, 'Where do I start?' and will help with breaking down *all* that you have to do into smaller units which you can actually manage.

WEEKLY ACTIVITY SCHEDULE

NOTE: Grade activities M for mastery and P for pleasure (0-10)

	Monday	Tuesday	Wednesday	Thursday	Friday	Saturday	Sunday
9-10	Had breakfast M4 P4	Had breakfast M4 P3					
10-11	Read papers M1 P0	Went back to bed M0 P6					
11-12	Shopping M6 P5	Sat about M0 P0					
12-1	Listening to Radio M5 P6	Prepared and had lunch M5 P5					
1-2	Lunch M6 P5	Read papers M3 P3					
2-3	Dosed M0 P2	Visit from my friend M5 P6					
3-4	Tidied up M6 P2	Talking to friend M5 P6					
4-5	Sat about M1 P4	Went down to the shops M5 P5					
5-6	Prepared Supper M4 P2	Prepared Supper M4 P2					
6-7	Had Supper M7 P7	Had Supper M4 P7					
7-8	Watched TV M6 P3	Talked on 'phone. Listened to records M8 P8					
8-12	Watched TV Went to Bed M5 P6	Watched TV Went to bed M6 P6					

Some tips about how to make your activity schedule work for you

Your schedule is just a guide, so you can be *flexible*. If something unexpected happens which disrupts your schedule, don't give up. A friend may call when you had planned to clean the bathroom, for example. You can use the visit as a distraction and try to enjoy it. The schedule can wait. You just continue with it when you can.

You may need to plan alternative activities as your plans may depend on factors beyond your control, such as the weather. So, if you cannot get on with the gardening, you can listen to that record you haven't had time to listen to yet, or indulge in some other pleasant activity. Your schedule is a general plan rather than prescribed hourly activities. If it is interrupted, don't try to go back to catch up, but just carry on and reschedule what you did not achieve for another time. Try to make plans which are not too general: 'cleaning the house', for example, is too general and 'weeding the garden' is probably too open-ended. If you tell yourself you *must* clean the entire house or weed the entire garden and you don't manage it, you'll probably think of yourself as a failure and get discouraged. On the other hand, if you simply set yourself the goal of cleaning or weeding for one hour, you increase your chances of success and how much you have achieved does not really matter. Above all, remember the saying: 'If something is worth doing, it's worth doing *badly*'. This may sound strange as it differs from what you have usually heard, but think about it. Isn't it worth cleaning the house less than perfectly, rather than not at all?

Review your schedule every evening to check your M and P ratings and how you got on. Did you schedule too much, or too little? Are you trying to run before you can walk? Do you need more pleasant activities? Were you blocked with negative thoughts? Can you write these thoughts out and challenge them as in the examples you read above? Were there other reasons why you could not keep to your schedule? Maybe you need to introduce some rewards for yourself after you've done a chore. For example, you may set time aside for a cup of tea; you may need more time to relax by listening to music or reading. It is important to balance your day evenly between pleasure and mastery.

8. Dealing with Negative Thoughts

Now that you've started working on your activities, you may have an increased sense of control and of achievement. Your mood may also have improved correspondingly. But you may still feel bad about yourself, about your world and your future. It is time to begin to look more closely at the thoughts which go through your mind when you have these sad, anxious or despairing feelings.

In the last chapter, we considered some of the thoughts which may block activity and, in Chapters 1 and 5, I described how, when depressed, people think negatively about themselves, their world and their future. This is sometimes called the *negative cognitive triad*. You saw examples of negative thinking in Chapter 6 and the type of logical errors we make when we think like this. Is there anything you can do about these thoughts? Are you thinking 'If this is the way I think, it means that's the way I am. I can't change my personality'?

The Negative Statements You Make to Yourself

Well, first of all, you don't think negatively about everything; most likely these distorted thoughts relate only to yourself, your relationships and situations which relate to you. Secondly, you have not been depressed all your life, so there have been times when you did not think in the same negative way. Thirdly, these negative thoughts do not reflect your personality; they are symptoms of depression, and symptoms, by definition, disappear if treated successfully. It is important to learn ways of dealing with these thoughts, because they maintain low mood and depressed behaviour.

The negative thoughts you must learn to 'catch' may not be easily accessible to you, because they are so habitual, that they have become 'automatic'. They just happen like a reflex action. You may not be aware that they are there. They are the running commentaries or 'self-statements' which go on at the back of your mind, while you may be engaged in some other activity. If you stop reading for a minute just now and listen to what's going on at the back of your mind, you may 'catch' a thought. Have you got it? Well, that's an 'automatic' thought. It indicates that you are able to read this book, take in what you're reading and at the same time have many other thoughts. Some sufferers have assured me that they don't think about anything, they just feel terrible. With careful questioning and training, we can usually access the thoughts which were there all the time, but had been taken for granted or ignored. Another characteristic of these automatic thoughts is that they are plausible. It does not occur to us to question them. If we think something, it must be true.

So, let us see how you can practise tracking the automatic thoughts which underlie depression, and then learn to challenge and modify them and to substitute more realistic and less negatively distorted ways of thinking.

How to Increase Awareness of Negative Thoughts

1. *Use a change in your feelings*

The first step is to become aware of what you are thinking. Since we are usually more aware of feelings and emotions than of thoughts, the easiest way to get at the thoughts is to use changes in your mood as cues. When you *feel* more sad or anxious or angry or hopeless or when you feel like crying, look at what's gone through your mind just before. You will find that over the course of a few days, you will become more sensitive to changes in your feelings and more aware of the thoughts which trigger off these feelings. What you may find is that the same thoughts occur again and again. This happens to us whether we are depressed or not. A famous scientist in the last century, Sir Francis Galton, decided to study his thoughts. While walking along Pall Mall, he would periodically record what he had been thinking and what objects along his route had triggered the thoughts. He wanted to show how these associated ideas 'though they are for the most part exceedingly fleeting and obscure, and barely cross the threshold of our consciousness, may be seized, dragged into the daylight, and recorded'. Sir Francis's main conclusion was that thoughts tend to recur, and his were mostly about the weather!

2. Count the thoughts

Another way of becoming aware of negative automatic thoughts is to count them. You can do that simply by totting up the thoughts on a wrist counter like those used by golfers, or by carrying a small card with you and making a mark on it for each thought that occurs. This method not only makes you more aware of the negative automatic thoughts, but it also allows you to stand back from the thoughts and observe them, so that their power to distress you is lessened. What may happen is that you may find that you are having more negative thoughts than ever. Don't be alarmed — this only means that you are getting better at catching them. They will become less frequent after a while. If you think 'If I have so many negative thoughts, it must mean that I cannot even think rationally. I must be inadequate and weak', remember that these thoughts are a sign of depression; they do not reflect your usual self. Would you label a fever in somebody who has influenza a sign of weakness?

3. Write them down

The next step to increase your awareness of how your negative thoughts bring on distressful feelings is to write them down as soon as you can after they have occurred. It may not be possible, for external reasons, to record your

thoughts and feelings immediately after they occur. You may be at work or out shopping or talking to somebody. If this is the case, just make a mental note of the feelings, the situations and the thought and write them down later. It is a good idea to set aside 20 minutes or so every evening for that purpose. The way to record your thoughts is to write down:

1.   What *emotion(s)* you felt and how bad it was, on say a scale of 0-100. It is useful to rate how bad the emotions are, as this would help you to differentiate between degrees of distress and to check whether you have been able to decrease the distress later. You will see some examples later in this chapter.

2.   Write down what *situation* you were in at the time. What were you doing precisely? This includes what you were thinking about. Just note this in general terms, just a few words will do.

3.   Then write down what *automatic thoughts* were running through your mind at the time. Try to record these thoughts exactly as they occurred to you. Some of these thoughts may come in the form of images rather than words. For example, you may have pictured yourself sitting on your own at home with no one to talk to. Describe exactly what you saw in the picture. Then, in the same way as you rated the strength of your emotions from 0-100, rate how far you believe in the automatic thought from 0-100. If you believe in the thought completely, you rate 100%. If you don't believe in it at all, you rate 0%. You could score anywhere between 0 and 100. The next crucial step is to challenge and modify the automatic thoughts.

How to Modify Depressive Thoughts

The reason why it is important to learn to become more aware of the automatic thoughts is so that you can then answer them and correct the biases that they contain, with the aim of improving your moods.

There are four major ways of challenging and correcting negative thoughts.

1. What is the evidence?

Do the facts of the situation support what you think completely or partially or do they contradict it? You meet a friend in the street who walks by without smiling at you. You think: 'Anne did not smile at me. I must have done something wrong to offend her'. A possible answer is 'It is true that she did not smile. What is the evidence that I did something wrong or that she is offended? It probably has nothing to do with me'.

2. Are there alternative interpretations which might be more realistic?

There are many different ways to look at any situation, as you have probably found when you have discussed some event with friends. So, list all the other alternatives that can explain the experience and review the evidence for and against each of them. You can then decide which alternative is most likely.

From the previous example: it may be that Anne did not smile because she did not see you; maybe she was preoccupied by problems of her own; maybe she was in a hurry and wasn't looking; maybe she was not wearing her glasses because she does not like to do so in public and she really does not see very well without them. Which of these alternatives is most likely relative to your original interpretation?

3. What is the effect of thinking the way you do?

How does it make you feel and how does it influence what you do? Can you find an alternative which will have a more positive effect? Your automatic thought may be: 'I've wasted so much of my life already. I should have dealt with my depression before'. A possible answer is: 'Brooding about the past does not help, it only makes me depressed. However, I can do something about the future.'

4. *What thinking errors are you making?*

You saw in Chapter 6 the different types of systematic errors that can distort your interpretations. So, look through the list and check whether you are overgeneralising or personalising or thinking in black and white or jumping to conclusions or catastrophising or disqualifying the positive or making 'should' statements. Many of these errors can occur in the same thought. Take, for example, the thought we looked at above: 'Anne did not smile at me. I must have done something wrong to offend her'. This thought contains both personalisation, Anne did not smile because of something you did, and jumping to conclusion, if she did not smile it must be because she was offended.

It is important to record and answer as many thoughts as possible each day. This technique allows you to become more objective. With practice, you will be able to do it in your head; but initially, the thoughts are too strong and you need to break the habit of taking the thoughts for granted.

1.   When you answer the automatic thoughts, write down all the answers you can think of and, as for automatic thoughts, rate your belief in them from 0-100.

2.   Once you have recorded all your answers, go back to the automatic thought and re-rate your belief in it now that you have answered it. You will probably find that your belief has decreased to some extent. If it hasn't, maybe you are disqualifying the answers in some way or you have not given answers which are convincing to you. If you note a disqualifying thought, write it down and answer it in the same way. Typical qualifying thoughts are — 'this is just a rationalisation' or 'it may apply to other people, but not to me'. Unhelpful challenges to the automatic thoughts are 'It's silly to think that' or 'I must try to be more positive'. Such answers are likely to make you feel worse because you are using more self-downing comments or you are just giving yourself

orders without any information about how to do it. Good answers take the automatic thought seriously and examine it in the four ways that were described in the previous section.

However, don't expect your belief in the negative thoughts to disappear completely at the first attempt. You have probably believed in them for a long time and the answer(s) may be quite new. Maybe you also need to test them out in action.

3. Now, you re-rate the original emotion as well. Remember you are doing this exercise to improve your mood and to relieve distressful emotions. Again, you will probably find that your painful emotions have decreased to some extent, but that they have not disappeared completely. Time and practice are needed.

4. *Finally*, you can ask yourself what action you can take, either to change the situation for the better or to test out the answers to the negative thoughts. How can you handle the situation differently next time? What will you do if you find yourself thinking and feeling the same way again?

How to record your automatic thoughts and your answers to them

The examples which follow are from the record sheets which I have collected during cognitive therapy sessions with depressed men and women of all ages and from all walks of life. They will illustrate the points discussed in the previous section and show you how to record the thoughts which accompany distressful feelings and how to answer them.

Some words of warning

Monitoring, questioning, evaluating and answering our thoughts is not something we normally do. Therefore, you may well find it difficult at first to tap into your thoughts, to be objective, and to find answers which actually help you to feel better. Do not be discouraged. This is a skill, like any other skill, which needs practice. So, give yourself a chance.

It is particularly difficult to find reasonable alternatives when you are feeling upset. In this case, just write the thought down and use some other method of improving your mood, for example, distraction and pleasant activities. Cheerful music has been found to be a particularly powerful method of changing moods. When your mood is a bit improved, you will find it easier to tackle the thought that you wrote down.

Your record is for your own benefit. It does not have to be a literary masterpiece. The right answer is the one which is helpful to you. No one answer will do for everybody.

Some people criticise themselves for having negative thoughts. Once they have written the thoughts down and answered them, they then say to themselves: 'I must be really stupid to think like that!' If this happens, write this thought down and answer it in the same way as you answered the original thought.

EXAMPLES OF AUTOMATIC THOUGHTS AND OF HOW TO ANSWER THEM

Situation	Emotion (rate degree, 0-100%)	Automatic Thoughts (rate belief, 0-100%)	Answers (rate belief, 0-100%)	Outcome (re-rate belief automatic thinking and emotion)
1. Wakened up, thinking about sale of house.	Anxious, sad (80%)	My financial affairs are in a mess. I shall not find another home in time. I should not have taken my lawyer's advice. (100%)	There are some difficulties because I need to find another house to buy in two months. But I am catastrophising when I say that my financial affairs are in a mess and I do not have a crystal ball to predict that I shall not find another home. My lawyer is experienced in these affairs and well placed to give advice. There are many houses for sale in the areas I want. It was a wise move to sell first in the current state of the housing market. (100%)	Automatic thought (30%) Anxious (30%)
2. Getting ready to go away for the weekend.	Angry (80%)	I'm just too tired to do any more. Why can't my husband help? (80%)	I am more tired than usual because of my depression. I don't need to pack tonight. John cannot read my mind. If I ask him, he will help willingly. (100%)	Automatic thought (0%) Sad (20%)

Examples of Automatic Thoughts and of How to Answer Them — contd.

Situation	Emotion (rate degree, 0-100%)	Automatic Thoughts (rate belief, 0-100%)	Answers (rate belief, 0-100%)	Outcome (re-rate belief automatic thinking and emotion)
3. Saw a friend at the bus stop and crossed the road to avoid talking to him.	Guilty (90%) anxious (90%)	I can't be bothered to talk to people. He may ask awkward questions and I won't know what to say. (100%)	I'm making negative predictions again. He has always been most understanding in the past. In any case, I don't have to answer his questions. Next time I see somebody I know, I'll just go up to them. If they ask awkward questions, I can give an evasive answer or say that I don't want to talk about that. It's an experiment that I can try. (60%)	Automatic thought (30%) Anxious (30%)
4. Talked to Dave on coming home from clinic.	Sad 50% frustrated 60%	He always seems to get the wrong end of the stick and he talks down to me as though I was a silly child. (100%)	I am overgeneralising and jumping to conclusions. Maybe I don't explain my feelings and thoughts clearly and therefore it is not surprising that he does not understand. I am interpreting his way of reassuring and comforting me as 'talking down to me'. Next time I'll try and explain more clearly. (80%)	Automatic thought (20%) Sad (30%)

Examples of Automatic Thoughts and of How to Answer Them — *contd.*

Situation	Emotion (rate degree, 0-100%)	Automatic Thoughts (rate belief, 0-100%)	Answers (rate belief, 0-100%)	Outcome (re-rate belief automatic thinking and emotion)
5. Visited mother.	Guilty, angry, depressed (100%)	If she had cared more for me, maybe I'd care more for her now. (100%)	She did possibly care, but, like me she cannot show her feelings. She showed she cared in other ways. I cannot show feelings now because I'm too depressed. When people are depressed, they cannot show their feelings for their family. It does not mean I don't love her. I'm just seeing everything in black at the moment. (100%)	Automatic thought (50%) Guilty, depressed (50%)
6. Children quarrelling about a television programme.	Angry (100%) Depressed (100%)	The children are really angry with me — not with each other, because I'm a rotten mother to them. (100%)	Children always quarrel about these things. My friends' children quarrel too. I'm personalising something that's got nothing to do with me. What's the evidence that I am a rotten mother? What is a rotten mother? I'll work out on another sheet evidence for and against the statement that I am a rotten mother. (80%)	Automatic thought (0%) Depressed (50%)

Examples of Automatic Thoughts and of How to Answer Them — contd.

Situation	Emotion (rate degree, 0-100%)	Automatic Thoughts (rate belief, 0-100%)	Answers (rate belief, 0-100%)	Outcome (re-rate automatic thinking and emotion)
7. Taking kids to film.	Anxious, depressed (90%)	I can't enjoy anything. I'm a useless father and a failure. (100%)	Lack of enjoyment is a symptom of depression. I'm not always like this. Even now, I can enjoy some things if I stop upsetting myself by calling myself useless and a failure. I know that I'm neither useless nor a failure. I'm good at my job and the children seem to enjoy doing things with me. (100%)	Automatic thought (30%) Anxious (50%)
8. Daughter tells me that bank phoned during the day. No coherent message.	Anxious (80%)	Something really important concerning our finances has happened. Poverty looms on the horizon. (80%)	Catastrophising, jumping to conclusions, fortune telling again. I just checked our bank balance last week and there was nothing wrong with it. It is more likely that I dated a cheque incorrectly. Ring and find out what the problem is — then you can do something about it. Can't solve imaginary problems. (100%)	Automatic thought (20%) Anxious (40%)

Examples of Automatic Thoughts and of How to Answer Them — *contd.*

Situation	Emotion (rate degree, 0-100%)	Automatic Thoughts (rate belief, 0-100%)	Answers (rate belief, 0-100%)	Outcome (re-rate belief automatic thinking and emotion)
9. Out shopping.	Sad (100%)	I'm losing this time. I can't fight back the depression any longer. (100%)	When I felt like this before, I tried some things which did help. I could phone a friend. It helps to talk when I feel like this. If my friend is out, I'll take a nice hot bath, relax and watch a film. Distraction helps. (100%)	Automatic thought (60%) Sad (50%)
10. After visit to the doctor.	Hopeless (100%) Disappointed (100%)	I am not getting any better. There is no future for me. The doctor probably thinks that I don't try hard enough. She is probably fed up with me. (100%)	I am disqualifying the positive. Compared to two months ago, I have made a lot of progress. I've just coped with a major life crisis. I would have crumbled before. There are still problems, but the doctor always takes time to talk to me and she told me I was doing well. She does not expect me to be 100% immediately. I am making the impossible demands upon myself, not the doctor. (100%)	Automatic thought (0%) Hopeless (10%) Disappointed (60%)

Examples of Automatic Thoughts and of How to Answer Them — *contd.*

Situation	Emotion (rate degree, 0-100%)	Automatic Thoughts (rate belief, 0-100%)	Answers (rate belief, 0-100%)	Outcome (re-rate belief automatic thinking and emotion)
11. Rang up a friend and her brother said she was out.	Sad (100%)	She must have told him to say she was out if I rang. (100%)	I'm jumping to conclusions and personalising. He sounded genuine, even told me where she'd gone. She's always been pleased when I rang before. There is no reason why she should want to avoid me. (100%)	Automatic thought (0%) Sad (30%)
12. Having a conversation with friends.	Insecure (100%) Depressed (100%)	I am totally incapable of any conversation. I am ignorant. (100%)	That's black and white thinking. I am generally as well informed as these people. They were talking about a technical matter to do with their work. If I don't know anything about that, it does not mean I am ignorant. If they don't know about my work, I don't think they are ignorant. It is unrealistic to expect to know everything about everything. (100%)	Automatic thought (30%) Insecure (50%) Depressed (20%)

Examples of Automatic Thoughts and of How to Answer Them — contd.

Situation	Emotion (rate degree, 0-100%)	Automatic Thoughts (rate belief, 0-100%)	Answers (rate belief, 0-100%)	Outcome (re-rate belief automatic thinking and emotion)
13. Jane did not turn up to play squash after I had really made the effort to get myself together and go.	Sad (100%)	She does not care about me. She does not like me; she didn't really want to go out with me. She only felt obliged. I'm a horrible person. (100%)	I am mind reading. She would not have made the arrangements if she did not want to play. She was not looking very well. She is probably too ill to play. (100%)	Automatic thought (20%) Sad (20%)
14. First day in new office. Didn't do very much.	Depressed (60%)	Oh dear! I'm dumb. I should have been able to organise myself better. (100%)	There are good reasons why I did not do more today. The office was in a mess. I still have to find out where things are and to work myself into the new system. Calling myself dumb is not helpful. There is no rule which says that people *should* fit into a new job immediately. This is an unrealistic expectation. What I can do, as I have difficulty at the moment organising myself, is make a list of things I could do tomorrow. (100%)	Automatic thought (30%) Depressed (20%)

Examples of Automatic Thoughts and of How to Answer Them — *contd.*

Situation	Emotion (rate degree, 0-100%)	Automatic Thoughts (rate belief, 0-100%)	Answers (rate belief, 0-100%)	Outcome (re-rate belief automatic thinking and emotion)
15. Sitting about in the evening.	Low (100%) Hopeless (100%)	How can I cope with my problems? There's no hope. (100%)	Yes, I have some decisions to take: about my apartment, my work, my girlfriend. At the moment, it all seems like one big unsurmountable problem because instead of taking a problem-solving attitude, I'm letting everything snowball. The way to solve problems is to break them down into small manageable components. So let's take my decision about work first — it's the most pressing. I'll write down all the alternatives which are open to me and work out the advantages and disadvantages of each alternative. Then I'll work out what actions to take. (100%)	Automatic thought (50%) Low (50%) Hopeless (10%)

Examples of Automatic Thoughts and of How to Answer Them — *contd.*

Situation	Emotion (rate degree, 0-100%)	Automatic Thoughts (rate belief, 0-100%)	Answers (rate belief, 0-100%)	Outcome (re-rate belief automatic thinking and emotion)
16. Woke up and kept thinking of office situation.	Disturbed, anxious, low (70%)	What mess am I going to have to go to? (70%)	I'm crystal ball gazing. It may not be a mess. However, if it is less well organised than before, it will be the responsibility of the supervisor. I can only do my work as well as I can and let other people worry about their work. (100%)	Automatic thought (10%) Anxious (20%)
17. Went into town on shopping trip.	Churned up inside and disappointed (75%)	I can't even cope with a little excursion. I had been feeling so well this morning and now I feel so tired and upset. I thought I had more energy than this. I have only been out for half an hour. I'll never get better. (75%)	This is the first time that I've been in town and it's another test which proves I'm not ready to cope with the hurly burly of town yet. I've been in quiet surroundings for some time. I'm still comparing my progress with a fully fit person instead of how much progress I've made in the past 2-3 weeks. (100%)	Automatic thought (20%) Disappointed (20%)

Examples of Automatic Thoughts and of How to Answer Them — *contd.*

Situation	Emotion (rate degree, 0-100%)	Automatic Thoughts (rate belief, 0-100%)	Answers (rate belief, 0-100%)	Outcome (re-rate belief automatic thinking and emotion)
18. Thinking about the past.	Sad (100%)	I've achieved nothing in my life. I've only ever disappointed my parents and let them down. I'm a failure. I hate myself. My life is worthless. What's the point? (100%)	I am selecting the negative and disqualifying the positive. I have passed my various exams. I did not get As, but I did get enough to do what I wanted to do. I did well in my first year at College. I am good at dealing with people. I have some of the qualities it takes to be a nurse. I am good at dealing with people. I have some of the qualities it takes to be a nurse. My parents have never said that they were disappointed with me.	Automatic thought (30%) Sad (50%)
19. Starting work again on Monday.	Anxious (60%)	What will I say if people ask what was wrong? People will probably think I'm not genuine, that I'm just lazy. (80%)	People know that I bend over backwards to be fair at work and I usually do more than my share anyway. I can make up for my absence by doing overtime. (70%)	Automatic thought (10%) Anxious (10%)

67

Examples of Automatic Thoughts and of How to Answer Them — *contd.*

Situation	Emotion (rate degree, 0-100%)	Automatic Thoughts (rate belief, 0-100%)	Answers (rate belief, 0-100%)	Outcome (re-rate belief automatic thinking and emotion)
20. Out with friends for a drink.	Anxious (70%) Low (60%)	It's important that they see that I am well. I've let them down by getting depressed again. (100%)	They asked me to come as I am; they did not say not to come if I was not completely well. They wanted to see me and it is unlikely that they will think that my depression has anything to do with them. It will be nice to see old friends. (100%)	Automatic thought (10%) Low (20%) Anxious (20%)

TWENTY QUESTIONS TO HELP YOU CHALLENGE NEGATIVE THINKING

1. *Am I confusing a thought with a fact?* The fact that you believe something to be true, does not necessarily mean that it is. Would your thought be accepted as correct by other people? Would it stand up in court, or be dismissed as circumstantial? What objective evidence do you have to back it up, and to contradict it?

2. *Am I jumping to conclusions?* This is the result of basing what you think on poor evidence. For instance, depressed people often believe that others are thinking critically about them. But none of us are mind-readers. How do you *know* what someone else is thinking? You may be right, but don't jump to conclusions — stick to what you know, and if you don't know, see if you can find out.

3. *What alternatives are there?* Are you assuming your view of things is the only one possible? How would you have looked at this situation before you got depressed? How would another person look at it? How would you look at it if someone else described it to you?

4. *What is the effect of thinking the way I do?* What do you want? What are your goals? Do you want to be happy and get most out of life? Is the way you are thinking now helping you to achieve this? Or is it standing in the way of what you want?

5. *What are the advantages and disadvantages of thinking this way?* Many distorted thought patterns do have some pay-off — that is what keeps them going. But do the disadvantages outweigh the advantages? If so, you can think out a new way of looking at things which will give you the advantages, but avoid the disadvantages of the old way.

6. *Am I asking questions that have no answers?* Questions like: 'How can I undo the past?' 'Why amn't I different?' 'What is the meaning of life?' 'Why does this always happen to me?' 'Why is life so unfair?'. Brooding over questions like these is a guaranteed way to depress yourself. If you can turn them into answerable questions, so much the better. If not, don't waste time on them.

7. *Am I thinking in black and white, all-or-nothing terms?* Nearly everything is relative. People, for instance, are not usually all good or all bad. They are a mixture of the two. Are you applying this kind of black-and-white thinking to yourself?

8. *Am I using global words in my thinking?* Watch out for words like always/never, everyone/no-one, everything/nothing. The chances are that the situation is actually less clear-cut than that. Mostly it's a case of sometimes, some people and some things.

9. *Am I condemning myself as a total person on the basis of a single event?* Depressed people often take difficulties to mean that they have no value at all as a person. Are you making this kind of blanket judgement?

10. *Am I concentrating on my weaknesses and forgetting my strengths?* When people become depressed, they often overlook problems they handled successfully in the past and resources which would help them to overcome current difficulties. Once they can change their thinking, they are often amazed at their ability to deal with problems. How have you coped with similar difficulties in the past?

11. *Am I blaming myself for something which is not really my fault?* Depressed people, for instance, blame themselves for being depressed. They put it down to lack of willpower, or weakness, and criticise themselves for not 'pulling themselves together'. In fact, scientists have been studying depression for many years and they are still not certain what causes it. Depression is a difficult problem to solve and blaming yourself for it will only make you more depressed.

12. *Am I taking something personally which has little or nothing to do with me?* When things go wrong, depressed people often believe that in some way this is directed at them personally, or caused by them. In fact, it may have nothing to with them.

13. *Am I expecting myself to be perfect?* It is simply not possible to get everything right all the time. Depressed people often set unrealistically high standards for themselves. Then they condemn themselves for making mistakes, or acting in ways they would rather not have done. Accepting that you can't be perfect does not mean you have to give up trying to do things well. It means that you can learn from your difficulties and mistakes, instead of being upset and paralysed by them.

14. *Am I using a double standard?* You may be expecting more of yourself than you would of another person. How would you react to someone else in your situation? Would you be so hard on them? You can afford to be as kind to yourself as you would be to someone else. It won't lead to collapse.

15. *Am I paying attention only to the black side of things?* Are you, for instance, focussing on everything that has gone wrong during the day and forgetting or discounting things you have enjoyed or achieved?

16. *Am I overestimating the chances of disaster?* Depressed people often believe that if things go at all wrong, disaster is sure to follow. If the day starts badly, it can only get worse. How likely is it that

what you expect will really happen? Is there really nothing you can do to change the course of events?

17. *Am I exaggerating the importance of events?* What difference does a particular event really make to your life? What will you make of it in a week, a year, 10 years? Will anyone else remember what you now see as a terrible thing to do? Will you? If you do, will you feel the same way about it? Probably not.

18. *Am I worrying about the way things ought to be, instead of accepting and dealing with them as they are?* Are you allowing events in the world at large to feed your depression? Telling yourself life is unjust and people awful? It is sad that there is so much suffering in the world and you may decide to do what you can to change things, but getting depressed about it does nothing to help.

19. *Am I assuming I can do nothing to change my situation?* Pessimism about the chances of changing things is central to depression. It makes you give up before you even start. You can't know that there is no solution to your problems until you try. Is the way you are thinking helping you to find answers, or is it making you turn down possible solutions without even giving them a go?

20. *Am I predicting the future instead of experimenting with it?* The fact that you have acted in a certain way in the past does not mean to say that you have to do so in the future. If you predict the future, instead of trying something different, you are cutting yourself off from the chance of change. Change may be difficult, but it is not impossible.

9. How to Be a Scientist in Your Everyday Life

You have seen in the previous chapter how you can challenge and argue against your negative automatic thoughts. However, this may not be enough to convince you that the thoughts are incorrect. You will need to build up a body of experience that contradicts them. The best way to do that is to act on your rational answers and test out in reality whether they are more realistic reflections of reality. Action helps you to break old habits of thinking and strengthens new ones.

People are like scientists. We make predictions and we act on them: 'If the light is green, I can drive through. The cars coming across will have stopped as the light will be red for them' 'If I do not water this house plant regularly, it will die'. These predictions are based on experience and they are *usually* right. Depressed people also make predictions and act on them, but these predictions are not based on experience; instead they stem from the negative bias in their thinking.

Testing your Predictions

Many negative thoughts take the form of predictions: 'I won't be able to cope', 'everyone will despise me', 'if I say what I think, people will look down on me'. When you question these thoughts, review the evidence, look for alternatives and take action to test them out, you are like a scientist running an experiment to test a new theory or hypothesis.

Examples

We will now examine actions which could follow from some of the examples given in the previous chapter.
(a)   Let's take Thought (3) which was written by Gill, a

secretary, who had been off work for three weeks because of depression. You can see that she still believed in her automatic thought at 30% after she had answered it. The thought was 'I can't be bothered to talk to people. He (friend) may ask awkward questions and I won't know what to say'. She was asked to write down her prediction clearly. This was: *If I talk to people they will ask awkward questions and I won't know what to say.*

We decided a plan of action to test the truth of her prediction.

Experiment 1   She would contrive a meeting with her friend. She would go out shopping at the same time as last time, as her friend, a work colleague, was usually at the bus stop at that time. Instead of crossing the road she would go up to him to greet him. She had written in her answers that she could give evasive answers or say that she did not want to talk about her depression. So, she could try one or both of these tactics.

Results: She did see the friend, went up to him and he did ask: 'How are you? When are you coming back to work?' These were the 'awkward' questions which Gill had feared. She gave a vague answer: 'Not too bad, should be back soon', but did feel acutely embarrassed. He did not pursue the subject and she left in a hurry.

Conclusions: Her prediction had been partly right. Her friend did ask a personal question and a vague answer worked partly. No more questions were asked, but she had felt bad. She recorded the thought which accompanied her feeling of embarrassment. 'He must think that I'm malingering, that there's nothing wrong with me'.

Prepare for *Experiment II*   Answer the negative thoughts which had crossed her mind during Experiment I. They included thinking errors such as mind-reading and jumping to conclusions. It may be more helpful to give a little bit more information, especially since it was a friend. To be able to do that she had to answer some other automatic thoughts: 'It is shameful to get depressed; depression is a sign of weakness'. Her answers to these thoughts were: 'Depression is an illness, not a sign of weakness. All sorts of people get depressed and they could not be described as weak. If some people think of it in that way, that's their problem. They need educating. I can't let their problem be visited on me'. Note that Experiment I helped to bring out important negative thoughts which interfered markedly with Gill's social behaviour and made her feel even more depressed.

Experiment II: Go to cafe where some of her office friends went at lunchtime and join them for a little while.

Results: This went well. When Gill disclosed that she was undergoing treatment for depression, somebody said that the same thing had happened to her two years previously, and somebody else talked about a relative who had been treated successfully for depression. Everybody was understanding and sympathetic.

(b) Thought (4) was written by Jane, a 35-year-old married woman; she thought that her successful husband, Dave, 'always gets the wrong end of the stick and talks down to me as though I was a silly child'.

Prediction: 'If I tell him how I feel, he will do what he did last time, he will say that it's a waste of time to see a psychotherapist, that what I need is something interesting to do'.

Experiment I Choose an appropriate time to talk to Dave, when he was not concentrating on some other activity or rushing off to work and tell him that she would like to talk to him about how she felt. We rehearsed what she could say and practised by role playing, that is, I played the role of Jane and she played the role of her Dave and then we reversed the roles, she played herself and I played Dave. The important points were:

1. To be empathic and understanding with her husband. He did not understand what it meant to be depressed; he was frustrated at not being able to help and maybe he was hurt, because he might feel that she did not care for him and for their home any more.

2. She would find some way of agreeing partly with what

he had said in the past, for example, it was true that she was doing nothing a great deal of the time, that it would help to start building up her activities and doing some of the things she used to enjoy.

3.   She would give him straight information about how she felt and what therapy entailed.

4.   She would try and involve him by working out together how he might help — for example, with her activity schedule and with her answering her negative thoughts.

Results: Jane was astounded by the response she got. Dave had thought that she was bored and that she was withdrawing love from him. He was very considerate when he understood how she felt and how depression can affect people. He showed interest in the therapy, which he thought was helping his wife in a practical way. They agreed that he could help by not expecting her to perform as she did before she got depressed, by making up weekly activity schedules with her and by prompting her to record and answer her thoughts if she started making excuses. Jane often felt unwilling to confront her thoughts. This can often be the case and is understandable, as it is quite natural to want to avoid painful experiences.

Conclusions: Her prediction had been wrong and her belief in the automatic thought was now 0%. What are the general lessons learned from this last experiment?

Action to Deal with Criticism

The general points which emerged and which applied to many other situations in Jane's life were how to deal with criticism, perceived or real. Sometimes, there is no implied criticism, but the depressed person sees criticism because of the negative bias in his or her thinking. In such a case, just answering the thoughts may be sufficient. But sometimes, there may be real criticism. Your family and friends may think that they can help you by pushing and exhorting you: 'Why don't you get out of bed?', 'You should try and do more', 'You should stop taking the medicine the doctor gave you and just get on with it'. This 'nagging' can increase your resistance and make you feel more depressed as it just emphasises the self-critical thoughts you have in your mind. Jane's method of dealing with the implied criticisms of her husband worked because she was using techniques which have been found to be very effective in dealing with criticisms. These are the steps that we practised in our role-play:

1.   *Empathy:* If somebody criticises you, they are probably trying to help you or to hurt you. Their criticisms may be either right or wrong. It is not helpful to start by attacking them back or to say nothing and become resentful or depressed. It is important to try and see what your critic really means, that is to try to see the *world* through his or her eyes. In the case of Jane and Dave, the conversation could have been:

> Jane: Dave, you said that I should stop seeing my therapist and do something interesting instead. What do you really mean by that?
> Dave: Well, you're moping about all the time. Seeing the therapist twice a week does not seem to help. It's a waste of time.
> Jane: How do you mean I mope about all day?
> Dave: You don't keep the house as tidy as you used to. You've stopped going to choir practice. You never see your friends any more.
> Jane: Yes, that's true. What else do you see that I've stopped doing?
> Dave: You're not taking as good care of yourself as you used to. You don't go to the hairdresser any more, you don't wear any make-up any more. You don't love me any more.
> Jane: But why do you think the therapist is not helping?
> Dave: You're not getting any better. I don't know what you talk about. Does she know how you are at home?
> Jane: I see, Dave, that I haven't kept you in the picture

and it is not surprising that you think that way. Let me try and tell you how I've been feeling and about my treatment.

By asking questions, Jane can find out how her husband perceives things. The more questions she asks, the more she and Dave can become aware of specific concrete problems which they can deal with. This tends to diffuse the undercurrent of anger and hostility and introduces a problem-solving attitude.

2. *Agreeing partly:* This is sometimes described as 'disarming the critic'. Jane could have attacked Dave by statements like: 'You always get the wrong end of the stick. You don't understand anything. You are inconsiderate'. This would make him even more resentful and a heated argument might have ensued. Otherwise, she could have left him and gone to another room, feeling unjustly criticised, misunderstood and in despair. The alternative was to agree partly with him. Whether the criticisms you encounter are right or not, the way to ease the situation is to find some way of agreeing with your critic. Jane had no difficulty in doing this. She could agree that she had stopped doing things, but not that the therapy was not helpful.

Jane: You are right. I have tended to let myself go and I have given up many things. I am sorry.

Dave: Is it me? You don't love me any more? Is the marriage on the rocks?

Jane: No, that's not it, Dave. I am suffering from depression. Depressed people lose interest in everything, they cannot do the simplest things any more, and what's worse, they can't show their feelings.

Dave: I'm sorry, Jane. I didn't mean to nag at you.

Jane: The therapist has given me something to read about depression. Maybe you would like to read that. She has been helping me to build up my activities gradually.

Dave: So, she is helping you in a practical way? I thought

> it might have been just a lot of mumbo jumbo. Is
> there something I can do to help?

By this time, Dave is no longer critical; he has given up the attack and he is beginning to be more understanding. Jane can now begin to discuss the changes she wants to bring about.

3. *Negotiation:* Once Jane had shown that she had listened to what Dave had to say, using the empathic method and she had prepared him for discussion rather than attack, by finding some way of agreeing with him, she could begin to explain her emotions and enlist his help in the treatment. Without making him feel ignorant or inconsiderate, she could explain the programme she was following in therapy, involve him partially in the treatment so that he could feel less helpless and, in particular, she was able to increase his understanding of what it means to suffer from depression. Thus, the techniques that she followed worked for her — she obtained the goal she wanted: more understanding and more help.

Following this plan to deal with criticism — empathy, disarming by agreeing partly and then negotiating — does not imply that you are not defending yourself if the criticisms are completely wrong-headed or even hostile. It does not mean that you cannot be angry. Anger is a perfectly natural and normal human emotion and it is a very powerful one for changing others' behaviour. The real point is how you express the anger. Angry outbursts may give a temporary feeling of relief, but they are not likely to help you attain your goal. They may disrupt your relationship with a person, put the other person on the defensive and make future interaction difficult. In the techniques described above, you just delay making your points, after showing empathy and partial agreement. If the criticisms are perfectly valid, however, you can just agree assertively with the criticism and thus gain the respect of your critic.

Sometimes you may feel that you simply have to let off steam because you feel so angry that you could not trust yourself to follow the techniques described above. This is perfectly understandable as anger can be a very strong emotion. In this case try not to do anything you would regret afterwards, for example breaking your best china or kicking the dog. Try something like punching your pillow or going for a ride on your bicycle or digging the garden. The relief at letting all this anger out can feel really good.

Summary: So, the best way of consolidating new interpretations or of changing depressing thoughts is to test them out in reality through action. You can gather information in books or by asking a sample of friends what they think about the subject which preoccupies you. You can attempt to do something in a different way to check whether you get better results. For example, if you are waking up in the night and finding it difficult to fall asleep again, you might be predicting each night when you go to bed: 'I'm going to wake up at 3.00 am and just lie and be miserable'. Why not test an alternative? 'Lying awake in bed increases my negative thoughts. If I get up and distract myself by reading or some other activity and then go back to bed, I might sleep better'. This is what a good scientist does, he tests out different alternatives.

10. Specific Problems

You have now learned techniques to organise and increase your daily activity level and you have found out ways to become aware of the thoughts which make you feel bad, and how to challenge and modify them. You are now ready to learn methods of dealing with some of the common problems which people who are depressed face. These are low self-esteem, sometimes even self-hate; a pervading sense of guilt and self-blame; hopelessness which makes you feel that life is not worth living; and difficulty in making decisions.

Low Self-esteem

All sufferers from depression, however successful or popular, or however many positive qualities others can see in them, find derogatory and self-critical things to say about themselves. They see themselves as lacking the qualities which they value; they think that they cannot reach their goals in life because of these defects; they consider that they are deservedly looked down upon, that they are unworthy and inadequate, that they are incapable or just not good enough and that they are rejects.

Let me give you some examples. Mary was an attractive middle-aged woman with a good marriage and two grown-up children whom she got on well with. She told me that she had avoided looking at herself in the mirror for the last 20 years, because she was so ugly. She never went to the hairdresser's, but cut her hair herself without looking in the mirror. Public lavatories were a problem because they usually have large mirrors and she had developed a series of clever tactics to avoid seeing her reflection. She put on her

make-up without looking in a mirror. It was surprising how successful she was at all this, as she looked very smart nonetheless.

Peter was a successful, highly respected, academic in his fifties. He was happily married, comfortably off and his two grown-up children had left home and had successful careers of their own, but kept in touch regularly with the family. Outside work, he had many interests, in particular, do-it-yourself activities in the house and sport. Peter never thought that he did anything correctly. As a professional, he felt that his work was not up to the standard he would like. He despised himself for not sitting on more committees and for avoiding giving public lectures which he thought he was very bad at. He was sure that his colleagues had no respect for him and that whatever he said was rejected or laughed at. In his private life, he criticised himself for being a bad husband and a bad father, a point of view his wife strongly disagreed with. In his activities around the house, he thought that he left too many jobs to pile up, that he could lay the wallpaper more neatly and attend to the garden more regularly. Peter even thought that he was the worst car driver about town.

Irene was a divorced woman in her early forties, with two young children at home. She had been feeling very depressed for many months and scarcely left her house. She was not afraid of going out, but she did not like to meet people. She thought that people looked at her with disgust because they could see what a despicable person she was. She loathed herself, called herself lazy, selfish and good for nothing. She considered that she was a bad mother and that it would be better for the children if they were taken away from her.

The examples could be endless, but you already see what these three individuals have in common: a general dislike for themselves, self-devaluation and self-criticism. This view of themselves is invariably accompanied by low mood, anxiety and sometimes anger. They really believe that they are worthless. How can that be? You may be thinking that the individuals in the three examples, Mary, Peter and Irene, are obviously not worthless, but that you know that *you* really are worthless. You feel inadequate and you know you're not as good as other people.

How to build a sense of self-worth

The first thing to do is to apply the techniques you have read about in Chapters 6, 7, 8 and 9. Try to write down exactly what you are saying to yourself. Your sense of worthlessness is maintained by your internal self-critical dialogue. Check from the list in Chapter 6 what type of thinking error you are making and then answer the thoughts, so that you can reach a more realistic view of yourself. The main thinking error which underlies low self-esteem is black and white or all-or-nothing thinking — you are probably using a simple two-way category: good-bad, capable-incapable, beautiful-ugly, when it comes to thinking about yourself. Do you think of other people in this way?

Let's go back to Mary who thought that she was so ugly that she could not look at herself in the mirror and reconstruct the conversation she had with me.

T: Do you have any features which are better than others?

Mary: No

T: Are you completely ugly, through and through?

Mary: That's what I think.

T: Is there anybody else more ugly than you?

Mary: I don't think so.

T: When you look at other people, do you make a judgement about their looks?

Mary: Well, that's the first thing that one notices about people.

T: You actually say to yourself, this is a beautiful person, this is an ugly person?

Mary: Not exactly.

T: What do you say to yourself?

Mary: I probably think they are more good-looking than I am.

83

T: You think they are more good-looking than you, but do you categorise them as either beautiful or ugly?

Mary: No.

T: So it looks as if you're using a different system when you judge other people? You put them along some sort of dimension, not in clear-cut categories?

Mary: That's right, I think 'she's got nice eyes' or 'she's got nice hair'.

T: If that's the way you think about other people, that people are not usually all beautiful or all ugly, how is it that you don't think about yourself in the same way?

Mary: Well I'm different, I'm really ugly.

T: Do you think that it may be possible that other people think about you the way you think about them?

Mary: Maybe.

T: Well, maybe we can collect some evidence about that. Is there anybody you know well enough you could talk to about the way you look? This is a difficult thing to do, but maybe you can ask your best friend, your daughters and your husband, for example. You could explain how you feel about your looks and ask a neutral question, such as, what are your best features and what are your worst features?

Mary I could try.

T. Okay, when we meet next week, you can let me know how you got on.

This example demonstrates low self-esteem often derives from the overstrict demands or rules or expectations that a depressed sufferer makes upon himself or herself while applying generally much kinder and more understanding rules when others are concerned.

The other typical error you are likely to be making when giving yourself self-critical labels is mind-reading or jumping to conclusions: because you think badly of yourself, you imagine that others do too. You know what the stranger in the street thinks; you know what your family really thinks, even though they say something different or even if you have never discussed the subject with them.

Thirdly, watch out for the 'should' statements that you are making to yourself. You are likely to be acting as an implacable task-master to yourself, never satisfied with what you actually do. You say to yourself: 'I should be a better mother', 'I should know that'.

Fourthly, you are probably also overgeneralising. Because you have made a mistake, you think that you always make mistakes and therefore that you are incapable and inadequate. Because you don't know something, you think that you are completely ignorant.

To build self-esteem you need to be a little kinder to yourself, to treat yourself as you would treat others. Try applying the same rules to yourself as you apply to others. The world is not made of two camps, with the rest of humanity on one side and you on the other. You are just as human as the rest of them, with some strengths and some weaknesses.

Guilt

Feeling guilty is one of the most common symptoms of depression. Depressed sufferers may brood about small errors they have committed in the past, they may think that they have committed unpardonable sins or crimes, that they are bad and deserve punishment. They may even think that the depression itself is a punishment. They feel responsible for causing distress to their family because they are ill, they blame themselves for everything which goes wrong, for getting angry or not getting angry, for others' unhappiness, for taking the doctor's time, in fact for everything bad. By contrast, they do not consider themselves responsible for good or positive events.

If you have been depressed you will have recognised these thoughts. They are related to the negative view of oneself as described in the previous section, but, in addition, they imply some moral codes which you have arbitrarily made up for yourself. You are prosecuting lawyer and judge, invariably reaching the verdict 'guilty' without having heard the defence lawyers. If you have an overwhelming feeling of guilt, ask yourself what you are blaming yourself for exactly.

Guilt implies having *done* something wrong, according to a moral or civil code of law. It usually means that somebody has chosen deliberately to harm or steal or lie or deceive, etc. In other words, it demands responsiblity and it requires a deed. You cannot be guilty of theft by sitting at home and fantasising about robbing a bank, can you? So, the first thing to remember is that you cannot be guilty for the thoughts that you have. You may feel so angry with somebody that you think to yourself 'I could kill him'. Are you then guilty of murder?

Secondly, when you feel guilty, ask yourself whether you are *responsible* for the negative event for which you are blaming yourself, and, if you are responsible, are you solely responsible or is the responsibility shared by others? For instance, let's imagine that you have a teenage son who is getting into trouble with the police. He goes around with a group of boys who have been caught sniffing glue. You say to yourself 'It's all my fault, I am a bad mother (or father). I should have kept a close eye on him'. Are you the only influence on your son's life? Is he a person in his own right, with friends and activities of his own? Is there peer group pressure? Has he a personality of his own? Does he go to school? All right, the answer is yes, you are not the only influence in his life. But, of course, you are the parent, so you have *some* responsibility, but you are not the only person to blame, if at all.

Blame, in fact, may not even be appropriate in the circumstance. If you blame yourself and feel 100% guilty, you will feel bad and this may stop you from dealing with the situation appropriately. There is a real problem — your son is indulging in behaviour which is harmful to himself and which may lead to further problems. If you stop blaming yourself, this will release more energy to look at the situation objectively and will enable you to be of more help to your son. You could investigate what is really going on, find out whether he is unhappy in some way; express your concern for him, advise and help him. If you find out that it is something to do with you — maybe your son thinks you do not care for him as you have paid less attention to him since you were depressed — you might then explain how you have been feeling and how depression affects you. You have paid less attention because you are depressed, not because you don't care, or because you are a bad parent.

Notice that in this example the thinking errors which increased the guilty feeling were not only 'personalisation', that is attributing the cause to yourself only, but also making a *'should'* statement. 'I should have kept a closer eye on him'. 'Should' statements are nearly always misplaced and they bring on guilt because you are breaking a rule that you have made up yourself. Try replacing 'should' with 'it would have been beneficial' or 'it would have been more helpful'. Ask yourself: 'Why should I? Who says so? What law says that?' and 'What is the usefulness of having such a rule?' Once you discover that one of these self-imposed rules is not helpful, you can modify it or get rid of it, since you made it up yourself. So, instead of saying 'I should be able to make my family happy', you might say 'It would be nice if I could make my family happy'. Instead of saying 'I should have known better', you could substitute 'If I could have foreseen the consequences, it would have been more useful to do something else'. 'Shoulds' often imply that you should have been able to know the future, as if you had a crystal ball that you *deliberately* did not consult.

Another typical error which increases guilt is *'catastrophising'*: 'I made a terrible mistake. They will never forgive me'; 'I should never have said that, I am a selfish, bad-tempered, no-good person'. Again, take your paper and pencil and work out how *terrible* the mistake was. So, you are not perfect, you made a mistake. Let's say you blamed friends for something they had not done. What can you do about it? You can apologise for your mistake, you can explain how the misunderstanding came about. If your prediction is right and they do not forgive you, is it your fault? Or is it rather that your friends have got a problem? If they expect you never to make a mistake, do you need to have the same expectation?

You can show *remorse* for doing something wrong and act accordingly, by apologising, acknowledging your mistake and making corrections where possible. Guilt is more likely to freeze your actions and be helpful neither to you, nor to others.

I am not, of course, saying that guilt is never appropriate. But, when you are depressed, the guilty feelings are either too intense and last too long, or they are a result of an excessive sense of responsibility, of excessive demand on yourself, of exaggerating the importance of some event, or of mistaking thoughts for actions. If you feel guilty, it does not mean that you are really guilty. You can examine the thoughts which make you feel guilty by using the sheet of automatic thoughts as shown in Chapter 8. Try to be fair, be the lawyer for the defence, as well as attorney for the prosecution.

Hopelessness

When you are depressed, you not only feel bad in the present and see yourself and your world in the most negative light, but you can remember most easily the sad and defeating events from your past. Moreover, when you look into the future, you see the current misery as going on for ever. So, you feel that there is no hope for you, you are in despair and may think 'What's the point? I would be better off dead'. You may even think of ways of terminating the pain; you may contemplate taking your own life or you might have made attempts at taking your life. Hopelessness is the component of depression which has been found to be highly associated with wishes to commit suicide and with attempts at committing suicide.

This extreme hopelessness is due to your negative way of looking at the future. You jump to the conclusion that there is only one solution to your problems; because your situation appears unbearable and unending, you erroneously conclude that suicide is your only escape. Although the conclusion may appear logical and reasonable to you, and you are thoroughly convinced that this is the only way out, I can assure you that you are totally wrong. You have seen from the examples given in this book how twisted our thinking can be when we are depressed. It is, therefore, imperative that you do not act in accordance with the thinking, especially when your life itself depends on it.

Real life problems

You may be thinking that the feeling of hopelessness is not necessarily based on erroneous thinking — your problems are real and you are having difficulties; bad health and loneliness are real problems, but the feeling of hopelessness which leads to the wish to die is not realistic. The hopelessness derives from your conclusion that there are no solutions and, by contemplating the final solution as it were, you are, in fact, blocking your problem-solving ability. Most problems can be solved, at least in part, and trying out solutions gives you a much needed sense of control.

A young woman, whose husband had just been made redundant, was so overwhelmed by what had happened, that she could see her children starving, the rent not paid and the bills accumulating. She thought that the whole family would be better off dead. Because she was depressed, she had not been able to work out solutions to her problem. When asked if she had consulted the Department of Social Security to see what help and benefits she was entitled to, she was surprised that she had not thought of such a simple solution. Could she take a part-time job to supplement the income if her husband was at home looking after the children? Could her husband take casual employment? How re-employable was he? After discussion with him, she reported that he himself was not worried about getting another job, as he was a skilled worker in the building trade. Sometimes solutions may not be as easy as in this case, but consulting your general practitioner or the local social services may help to put you in touch with organisations which can help, be they marriage guidance counsellors, women's groups, community groups and so on. The important thing to remember is to talk about feelings and to look for help if you yourself cannot think of solutions.

Advantages of living

Many sufferers who have contemplated or attempted suicide have told me that, with hindsight, they cannot understand how they came to see their life with such a pessimistic outlook. The arguments which appeared compelling are no longer so and they are glad to be alive. There are many errors in your thinking which lead to a pessimistic outlook. You *jump to conclusions* and believe that you are a *fortune teller*. You get the crystal ball out again and foresee for yourself the blackest future. You *catastrophise* your current problems, *undervalue* your ability to cope and *filter out* positive aspects of your present and past life.

To tip the balance in favour of living and against the wish to die, it is useful to do a simple exercise. Take a sheet of paper and write down what you gain by dying and what you lose by dying. On another sheet, write down the advantages of living. The example which follows is that of Tom, a man of 43 years, married with two children. Tom was in full-time employment as a mechanic and he had, two years previously, been in hospital for treatment of depression. He was currently depressed, but could continue working. He attended the hospital once a week for cognitive therapy. He thought: 'I would be better off dead' because he found life a continuous struggle. He slept badly, felt a band round his head, had difficulty concentrating and he had lost interest in all his leisure activities.

Tom did the following exercise to examine his belief that he would be better off dead.

Pros of dying	*Cons of dying*
1. I won't feel depressed any more.	1. I will miss seeing my family grow up.
2. I will have peace of mind.	2. If I had killed myself, I would have missed seeing my daughter going to school.
3. I won't have to live a life of pretence any more.	3. I would miss having holidays with the family.
	4. I have had some good moments in the last four years.
	5. My dying will affect the children's lives.
	6. There are many things I can do and enjoy doing: gardening, working on car, helping people.
	7. If I die, I miss the opportunity of getting better.

The advantages of living for him were:

1. Make sure my family is happy and well provided for.

2. Enjoy activities: gardening, social occasions with friends, swimming with the children, tinkering with car, working.

Tom's wish to die decreased significantly when he had worked out that it was to his advantage to live. He worried that the impulse might come back, but thought that it would be helpful to re-read what he had written if the suicidal thoughts came back.

Another common reason that sufferers give for their wish to die is not only that they would be better off dead, but that their family would be better off without them. Ask yourself, whether they would really? Your family may be distressed because you are unhappy, but would they be happier if you were dead?

Isn't the very fact that they are distressed by your suffering an indication that they care? And if they care, how would they feel about you taking your own life?

Although even individuals who are not depressed do have occasional suicidal thoughts, remember that when you are depressed, suicidal impulse is a dangerous symptom.

The points to remember are: do not be embarrassed to talk about it with your doctor — there is no shame about feeling hopeless; you would only be reporting a symptom of depression. You can answer your unrealistic hopeless thoughts by adopting a problem-solving attitude. It is useful to make a balance sheet of the pros and cons of dying and the advantages of living to try and redress the balance in your mind. A counsellor or therapist could help you, if you have difficulties in filling in the positive side or if you do not know alternative solutions to your problems. Remember, above all, that depression is self-limiting and that there are a number of effective treatments which your doctor can prescribe. If you and your doctor feel that you cannot exercise enough control at a particular time, you can go into hospital for a short while, for your own protection, until your symptoms improve.

Indecision

Sometimes depressed sufferers feel that something has happened to their brain because they cannot think clearly, their thoughts are slow and muddled and they cannnot make the simplest decisions. You can be assured that there is nothing physically wrong with your brain; these are frequent symptoms of depression which will disappear when you recover.

The difficulty in making decisions is often related to lowered self-confidence. You don't trust yourself to make the right decisions any more because you feel so inadequate. You may believe that you have lost all ability to make decisions. Some sufferers describe how they cannot decide what to do first and how they often start one thing, then switch to another and another, so that they end up in a complete muddle. You saw in Chapter 7, how you can plan your activities using a daily activity schedule. This technique is helpful for everyday decisions which you may have difficulties with because of the slow and muddled thinking which accompanies depression.

For bigger decisions, you need a different approach. Try writing down all the different alternatives which are open to you, then write down all the pros and cons which each alternative offers. Having done that, give a plus value from 0 to 100 to each pro and a minus value from 0 to 100 to each con and then add up all the pros and all the cons. Thus each alternative, at the end, has an overall plus or minus value and you can decide which alternative serves your advantage best. Let me give you an example.

Susan is married and she has two children aged 6 and 8. She had stopped working when the children were born and had gone back to work two years ago, as a manageress in an insurance office. Her husband is a successful administrator in the civil service. Since going back to work, she had suffered a severe depressive episode from which she had recovered after an admission to hospital. She could not decide whether she should go back to her full-time job, which she used to enjoy. Her husband, parents and in-laws were under the impression that the work was too much for her and had been the cause of her depression. She had a house to look after, a husband and two young children. Friends and colleagues made her feel *guilty* for not looking after her children. Susan commented: 'They may be right; what's the point of having children if you don't look after them?'.

What was Susan to do? She thought she had four alternatives: go back to the same job, full-time as before; go back to the same job on a part-time basis; look for another part-time job which was less demanding, or not go back to work at all. She worked out the pros and cons of each alternative as described above.

Alternative I: Go back to the same job on a full-time basis as before

Pros	Cons
1 I enjoyed the job, because of its responsibility (80)	1 It was not a 9 am - 5 pm job, so I never knew when I would get home and sometimes I had to take work home with me (100)
2 I knew the job and could do it well (80)	2 The pressure might make me ill again (100)
3 If I got depressed again I could have time off without prejudice to my job, as the employers had been very understanding the last time (100)	3 It was not fair on the children not to spend more time with them (100)
4 It gave me a good income of my own and made me feel independent (20)	
————	————
+280	−300
————	————

Against −20: This alternative is on the whole more disadvantageous than advantageous.

Alternative II: Go back to the same job on a part-time basis

Pros	Cons
1 It would give me more time with the children (100)	1 I would no longer have the responsibility which I enjoyed (80)
2 Since I don't need the full income anyway, the part-time income would still make me feel independent (20)	2 It is a difficult job to do part-time. I might find myself doing as much as before for less money (80)

3 It would be less pressure
and I might feel better
(100)
4 I would be able to move
to full-time again when
the children are more
grown up (100)

+320   −160

For +160: This alternative is more advantageous

Alternative III: Look for another part-time job which is less demanding

Pros	Cons
1 It would involve regular hours — more time at home (100)	1 Better the devil you know. A new job might turn out inappropriate (80)
2 May be less interesting, but would get me out of the house nonetheless (60)	2 I get bored by routine jobs (80)
3 My husband would be happier with this (50)	3 Less money (20)
4 Less pressure would be better for my health (100)	

+310   −180

For +130: This alternative is also more advantageous.

Alternative IV: Not go back to work at all

Pros	Cons
1 A lot of free time to do things with the children (100)	1 I would miss having an interesting job outside the home (100)

2 I could use the spare time at home to study a language or something else (30)

2 I would be bored (50)

3 I could spend more time on my hobbies: gardening, cooking, going out with friends (20)

3 I would be resentful (50)

4 Both sets of parents and my husband would approve (50)

4 In nine years time, by the time children have grown up, I will be older and it would be more difficult to get into the job market (20)

5 May be better for my health (100)

―――――
+300
―――――

―――――
−220
―――――

For +80: This alternative is similarly more advantageous.

At the end of this exercise, Susan found that:

Alternative I was more unfavourable: − 20
Alternative II was more favourable: +160
Alternative III was more favourable: +130
Alternative IV was more favourable: + 80

Therefore, on balance, going back to the same job on a part-time basis was more favourable. This way of dealing with important decisions helps you to work out the various arguments which go round in your mind in a rational manner, but it also decreases anxiety and it becomes obvious that no decision is all good or all bad. There are good points and bad points and all you can do is work out as best you can the balance which is most advantageous or most useful to you at a particular time. Another point to remember, which will also reduce your anxiety when you have a decision to take, is that most decisions are reversible.

Decisions can therefore be regarded as experiments. If they turn out to be the wrong decisions, that is if they do not work out, you can try something else.

The technique I have described above can be applied to all sorts of situations, even everyday ones, for example should you watch television tonight or get on with a piece of work? This decision may involve three important aspects: peace of mind, efficiency and social aspects. Rate the two alternative decisions for the importance of each aspect for you and for the pleasure you would get. Here is another example, this time using a scale of 0-10 for importance (I) and for pleasure or lack of pleasure (P) and multiplying the two ratings.

Prepare college work

Pros	*Cons*
Peace of mind Will feel good about making a start	Will start worrying about college and not sleep well
$I5 \times P8 (+40)$	$I7 \times P4 (-28)$

Balance = $+12$

Efficiency Less work to do over whole week and will be better prepared	Will be less fresh to-morrow: will do less over whole week
$I9 \times P5 (+45)$	$I6 \times P7 (-42)$

Balance = $+3$

Social Can have chat with friend when I finish	Shutting myself away in room is anti-social
$I5 \times P5 (+25)$	$I6 \times P6 (-36)$

Balance = -11

Overall balance = $+4$

Watch film on television

Pros	Cons
Peace of mind More pleasant, relaxing evening I4 × P7 (+28)	Film may be boring and I will feel guilty about not working I5 × P3 (−15)

Balance = +13

Efficiency I'll feel fresh to-morrow I6 × P7 (+42)	Wasting time now means I will have too much to do next week I7 × P5 (−35)

Balance = +7

Social I can talk to my friend I5 × P7 (+35)	She is likely to be busy in her room I4 × P4 (−16)

Balance = +19

Overall Balance = +39

The conclusion is that both options are good, but on the whole, it is better to watch the film.

In summary, the different sections of this chapter have given you some ways of coping with some of the main symptoms of depression. These techniques will not make the depression go away immediately or completely, but they will increase your sense of control and, therefore, your confidence in yourself. Little by little, as you find that you can solve some of these problems, you will also experience an improvement in the way you feel.

11. Attitudes Which May Make You Depressed

When you are feeling much better, the painful feelings have gone, you are now active and interested, your sleep is improved and all the other symptoms have disappeared.

The depression belongs to the past and you don't want to think about it. This is completely understandable, but you may wonder: 'How could I think like this before? What made me see life in such a black light?' You saw in Chapter 2 that there can be many different causes of depression, and it is difficult to pin-point a cause for an individual. There are, however, basic beliefs or attitudes which, if held very strongly, can make you more likely to become depressed. These may have become apparent to you when you started keeping note of your automatic thoughts and from the examples in the previous chapters. These attitudes are sometimes called 'silent assumptions', because you are not fully aware that you have these personal rules by which you define your worth. They are, if you wish, your personal philosophy or the invisible glasses through which you look at the world and reach interpretations and conclusions.

Examples

Here are 15 examples of personal rules which can lead you to have frequent negative experiences and consequently to have negative thoughts about yourself and negative feelings.

1   I should always put other people first — not to do so is selfish.
2   I should be happy all the time.
3   If I cannot do something well, there's no point in doing it at all.
4   If I ask a question, people will think I am stupid and inferior.
5   It is shameful for a person to show any sign of weakness.
6   If I am alone, I will inevitably be lonely and miserable.
7   If someone is better than me at something, that means he or she is a better person than me.
8   Unless I am loved, I cannot be happy.
9   If someone dislikes me, that means I am not likeable.
10   It is better to do nothing than to risk making a mistake.

11   Unless things turn out as I want them to, my life is wasted.

12   Unless I set myself the highest possible standards, I am likely to be second-rate.

13   My worth as a person depends on what others think of me.

14   If I do well, it's probably due to chance: if I do badly, it's probably due to me.

15   If I disagree with someone, they won't like me.

Rate your belief on a 0-100 per cent scale in each of these examples and you will get some idea of your area of vulnerability.

Characteristics

Note that these attitudes are often phrased as strict and rigid rules: they use terms such as 'should', 'always', 'unless' and 'nothing'. They are black and white rules, with no shades of grey, it's either 100% or nothing. They relate to themes of approval, love, perfection, criticism, achievement, omnipotence and entitlement, that is what is owed to you by others. It is likely that you have learned these attitudes in your childhood, perhaps from your parents or teachers, and as you grew up, although you changed most of your childhood beliefs, some remained unchanged.

You may be feeling discouraged at this point, thinking 'If these beliefs have been there for so long, they cannot be changed. There's nothing I can do. It's my personality'. In therapy, we find that it is not so and we have evidence that change does occur as people who have had cognitive therapy appear to become less vulnerable to future depressions.

How to Become Aware of Depressive Attitudes

To be able to change or weaken these beliefs, you have first of all to become aware of what depressive attitudes you have. The list you have just checked will have given you some idea, but there are other methods you can use to find what is relevant for you as an individual, in your own words.

Remember that as these beliefs are 'silent', you are not able straight off to say what they are. Your thoughts, interpretations and mental images are more available to you. In the previous sections, you practised catching your automatic thoughts and keeping a record of them. Now take a sample of these thoughts and ask yourself what belief or attitude they might reflect. Are the main themes related to being loved by most people? Have you generally felt depressed when you thought people were criticising you or disapproving of you? Do words relating to performance or achievement recur most often? Have you generally felt down when you thought people were being unfair to you or not dealing with you the way you are entitled to? Do the thoughts refer primarily to self-criticism because you had made mistakes?

So, the main themes of your automatic thoughts will indicate to you what your depressive personal rule(s) is or are. Then try and write down exactly what the rule appears to be that made you think the way you did.

Another method which you might try to help pin-point your 'silent assumption' is the downward arrow technique. Take a depressing automatic thought and work out what it implies for you. Let us take some examples from the thoughts listed in Chapter 8.

Example 11, page 63 was:

Situation: Rang up a friend and her brother said she was out
Emotion: Sadness (100%)

Automatic Thoughts		*Answers*
She must have told him to say she was out if I rang	→	

1. 'If she *did* say that, why
   ↓ would it be upsetting to
   me?'

2. It would mean that she   →
   did not like me.
   'Suppose this is true,
   ↓ she does not like me,
   what would this mean
   to me?'

3. It would mean there's   →
   something wrong with
   me. Otherwise she
   wouldn't try to avoid
   ↓ me.
   'Suppose this is true,
   what would that mean
   to me?'

4. It would mean that   →
   people would not want
   to have anything to do
   with me.
   ↓ They would reject me.
   'And if that were true,
   what would it mean to
   me?'

5. It would mean that I   →
   was unlovable, totally
   worthless.
   ↓ 'And if that were true,
   what would it mean to
   me?'

6. It would mean that my   →
   life was not worth
   living. I would be
   miserable.

Thus by pursuing the meaning of the automatic thoughts, you reach your personal rules:

Basic Assumptions: I must be liked by everybody. If somebody does not like me this means I am unlovable and worthless and life is not worth living

Notice that when you are following the downward arrow technique, you are doing the opposite of what you learned to do when answering depressing automatic thoughts. Instead of substituting more reasonable answers, you are pursuing the personal meaning of the automatic thoughts to their final point, as if the automatic thoughts were valid. However, after you have done that, remember to answer the automatic thoughts by re-examining them for errors and by challenging them.

Example 14, page 64.

Situation: First day in new office. Didn't do very much.

Emotion: Depressed (60%)

Automatic Thoughts		Answers
1. Oh dear! I'm dumb, I should have organised myself better	→	
↓ 'Suppose that were true; I should have organised myself better. Why is this so upsetting to me?		
2. It means that I can never get things right or do things properly	→	
↓ 'Suppose that were true; what does it mean to me?'		
3. It means that people would not trust me to do anything perfectly.	→	
↓ 'Suppose that were true; what would it mean to me?'		

4. It would mean that I   →
    am second-rate, useless.
    ↓ 'Suppose that were true,
    what would it mean to
    you?'

5. It would mean that I   →
    am worthless, just a
    flop. Nobody would
    respect me.

Basic Assumptions: (1) *I must do everything perfectly, if not, I am worthless;* (2) *If I do not do things perfectly, people will not respect me.*

Example 19, page 67.
Situation: Starting work again on Monday
Emotions: Anxious (60%)

       Automatic Thoughts   *Answers*

1. What will I say if people ask   →
    what was wrong? They will
    probably think that I'm not
    genuine, that I'm just lazy.

    'Suppose they do think
    ↓ that. Why is it so upset-
    ting to me?'

2. People will be criticising me   →
    or laughing at me.

    'Suppose this were true.
    ↓ What would it mean to
    me?'

3. They would think I'm no   →
    good; just a fake.

    'Suppose that were true,
    ↓ what would that mean
    to me?'

4. It would mean that I am no → good and inferior.

↓ 'Suppose that were true, what would that mean to me?'

5. It would mean that people → would not like and respect me. I would be dismissed as a nobody.

Basic Assumptions: My worth depends on the approval of others. If somebody disapproves of me or thinks badly of me, it means I am worthless.

The three examples we have just looked at, possibly with some modification for different individuals, are the most common basic attitudes which can make people vulnerable to depression: the need to be loved or liked by everybody; the need to do everything perfectly all the time or the need to get it right each time; and the need for approval or respect from everybody.

It is important to note that most of us have these attitudes to a *certain degree*. We prefer to be liked than to be disliked; it is more rewarding to get something right than to get it wrong, to do something well rather than badly; and it is more pleasant to be approved of and respected, than to be criticised or dismissed. However, in the case of people who become depressed, they hold these attitudes too strongly and too rigidly. This means that they are open to more negative experiences and they are more likely to misinterpret situations as dislike, failure or disapproval, because they are constantly on the lookout for such situations.

How to Modify Attitudes

Often by just *bringing these beliefs into the open*, by making them explicit, you can judge better how extreme and inappropriate they are. This process, in itself, will weaken their strength and make you query their validity.

Secondly, by answering each automatic thought in the downward arrow technique, as illustrated above, you will challenge the beliefs and make them more flexible and less encompassing. Let us look at how this can be done using the same examples.

I Automatic Thoughts	*Answers*
1. She must have told him to say she was out if I rang.	I'm jumping to conclusions and personalising. He sounded genuine, even told me where she'd gone. She's always been pleased when I rang before. There is no reason why she should want to avoid me.
2. It would mean that she did not like me.	Even if she did not feel like seeing me today, it would not mean that she did not like me. She may be unwell or otherwise engaged and got her brother to say a white lie to avoid hurting my feelings. Our friendship goes back a long way and I have a lot of evidence that she likes me.
3. It would mean there's something wrong with me. Otherwise she wouldn't try to avoid me.	If she avoided me, it could be for many reasons, mostly to do with herself. Even if she thought there was something wrong, it would not mean that there is something really wrong with me. Her opinion does not make it a reality.

4. It would mean that people would not want to have anything to do with me. They would reject me.

Different people like different things and like different types of people. If one or more individuals do not like me, it does not mean that the whole of humanity would reject me.

5. It would mean that I was unlovable, totally worthless.

Neither my friend nor anybody else has the prerogative to judge who is lovable and who isn't, who is worthless and who isn't. My worth as a person depends on what I am and what I do, not on what other people think. After all, I can think of one or two people whom I definitely do not like and this does not make them worthless.

6. It would mean that my life was not worth living. I would be miserable.

It is impossible to be liked by everybody because people have different likes and dislikes. There are many different worthwhile aspects to my life which have nothing to do with whether A or B likes me. If I concentrate on these and enjoy the company of people who like me and whom I like, I will not feel miserable.

II Automatic Thoughts

Answers

1. Oh dear! I'm dumb, I should have organised myself better.

There are good reasons why I did not do more today. The office was in a mess. I still have to find out where things are and to work myself into the new system. Calling myself dumb is not helpful. There is no rule which says that people *should* fit into a new job immediately. This is an unrealistic expectation. What I can do, as I have difficulty at the moment organising myself, is make a list of things I could do tomorrow.

2. It means that I can never get things right or do things properly.

I am overgeneralising. I do get things right sometimes. In fact, my work is highly praised. Because today was not very productive, it does not mean that I never get things right.

3. It means that people would not trust me to do anything perfectly.

Wait a minute, what is perfection? Can perfection exist in reality? People do not expect me to do things perfectly. I expect it of myself and this is demanding the impossible.

4. It would mean that I am second-rate, useless.

Getting things wrong sometimes or not doing things perfectly does not make me second-rate. In any case, being second-rate would not make me useless through and through. Like other people, I can do some things better than others. I am a human being with some good qualities and

some not so good. To err is
human, as they say.

5. It would mean that I
    am worthless, just a flop
    Nobody would respect
    me.

My worth cannot depend on
doing everything perfectly.
If getting things right all the
time defined somebody's
worth, then everybody
would be worthless as everybody makes mistakes. If
somebody loses respect for
me because I've made a
mistake, then that's his
problem, not mine. I
tolerate mistakes in other
people and do not lose
respect for them. It's time I
start treating myself as I
treat others.

III Automatic Thoughts   *Answers*

1. What will I say if people
    ask what was wrong?
    They will probably
    think I'm not genuine,
    that I'm just lazy.

People know that I bend
over backward to be fair at
work and I usually do more
than my share anyway. I
can make up for my absence
by doing overtime.

2. People will be criticising
    me or laughing at me.

I am mind-reading. When
other people have been off
sick before, I never heard
any negative criticism or
ridiculing.

3. They would think I'm
    no good; just a fake.

It does not make sense to
think that people will reach
such sweeping conclusions
about me because I have
been off sick for three days.
Did I think like this when X
was off with influenza
recently? No, I did not.

There is no reason to think that others will think this about me. If some of my colleagues do jump to such conclusions about me, *they* would be making the thinking errors. Their thoughts or interpretations cannot harm me.

4. It would mean that I am no good and inferior.

If somebody thinks that I am no good, this does not mean that I *am* no good. Last week, I thought how ignorant John was because he did not know a simple procedure at work. I realised afterwards that I was making a sweeping judgement on him. And then, I thought my judgement did not detract in any way from his worth. It's the same in my case. Somebody's thoughts cannot decrease my worth.

5. It would mean that people would not like and respect me. I would be dismissed as a nobody.

In the first place, everybody does not approve of the same thing. Somebody may approve a particular action which is frowned upon by somebody else. It is impossible to be approved of by everybody. Secondly, I am assuming that people would lose respect for me and not like me, if they found that I had some flaw. Let me look at the people that I like and respect. Do they have any characteristics that I consider as weaknesses or that I do not approve of? Yes, of course; there is no reason to assume that other people are different from me.

These examples may not fit your own particular beliefs or assumptions, but if you use the same techniques, you will be able first to find out what the beliefs are and then to use your own reasoning ability to examine them. You can also enlist the help of a friend or relative to help you with the answers.

There is a *third method* you can use to challenge your basic rules: this is to work out how useful they are to you. What are the advantages and disadvantages of keeping that particular rule? What are the costs and benefits? If you find that the rule is mostly to your disadvantage, you will be more inclined to modify it. We can go back to the same three examples for the sake of illustration.

Example I   *Basic Assumption: I must be liked by everybody. If people do not like me, this means that I am worthless.*

Advantages of this belief	*Disadvantages of this belief*
1. It makes me behave nicely to everybody.	1. It makes me vulnerable to different people's likes and dislikes.
2. People will think well of me.	2. Since people are different, I have to be many different things to different people, trying to please everybody at once.
3. I can have many friends.	3. I find myself doing things I do not really want to do just in order to please people.

4. I cannot express my own opinion in case it displeases somebody.

5. I need constant reassurance as I cannot always tell whether somebody likes me or not.

6. If somebody is in a bad mood and is not being particularly nice, I think that it's something to do with me and I feel bad.

7. It makes me avoid social situations in case people do not like me.

8. Since it is impossible to be liked by everybody, I put myself in a no-win situation which gets me depressed.

Example II   *Basic Assumption: I must do everything perfectly, if not, people will not respect me and I am worthless*

Advantages of this belief	*Disadvantages of this belief*
1. It makes me try hard to do well.	1. It increases my anxiety, so that my performance suffers.
2. It makes me produce good work and be successful.	2. It stops me from doing many of the things I would like to do, because I may not succeed.
3. When something goes well, I feel really good.	3. It makes me very critical of myself, so that I cannot take pleasure in what I do.

4. I cannot afford to let my mistakes be noticed by anyone, and therefore I probably miss out on valuable constructive comments.
5. When I get criticised, I become defensive and angry.
6. My successes are undermined, because any subsequent failure wipes out their significance.
7. I become very intolerant of others. I find so many faults in others, that I cannot be warm and friendly. I will end up without any friends.
8. I can never think well of myself because it is impossible to get it right all the time.
9. Because I get so upset by failures, I cannot use them as valuable experiences to learn how to do things better the next time.

Example III *Basic Assumption: My worth depends on the approval of others; if somebody disapproves of me or thinks badly of me, it means that I am worthless.*

Advantages of this belief
1. It makes me try and do things correctly at work.

Disadvantages of this belief
1. It makes me excessively self-conscious. I am always watching other people to assess what they think of me.

2. It makes me considerate towards others.

2. It makes me less assertive than I could be in certain situations and then I feel that people are taking advantage of me.

3. It makes me popular.

3. It makes me keep aloof from people, in case they get to know me better and find out about my faults.

4. I can only be comfortable with a few people I know very well, my family and my girl-friend, as I have to be on the watch with everybody else.

5. I cannot afford to say what I think in case it is not the right thing.

6. At work, I get very anxious in case my colleagues think that I am not doing something correctly.

7. Nearly every day, somebody says something that I interpret as criticism or disapproval and this makes me feel depressed.

8. I avoid doing something that I have not done before, in case I do not do it well.

> 9. If I do not know
>   something, I cannot ask
>   somebody in case they
>   think I'm ignorant or
>   ineffectual or ridiculous.

These three examples of cost-benefit analysis showed to the sufferers who wrote them out that their basic rules were working against them, on the whole. There were some benefits, but the cost was too high and it was to their advantage to relax the rules.

Finally, there is a *Fourth method* which you can use to challenge the validity of your basic assumption, once you have worked out what it is. As described in Chapter 9, it involves making a test. This time, you deliberately act against your belief to test whether your assumed predictions are true. Rules imply negative consequences if they are not followed. For example, 'You should not commit murders' implies that if you do commit a murder, you will be apprehended and tried for a crime; 'You should not drive on the motorway at speeds exceeding 70 miles per hour' implies that if you were stopped by the police, you could be charged for committing an offence.

Similarly, when you say to yourself 'I must be liked by everybody', you are predicting that 'If I do something which somebody does not like, that person will reject me, I will lose their friendship, I will be rejected by everybody, I will end up alone without a friend in the world'. You may set up a situation where you break your rule, you do something or say something which is likely not to please a friend. You might turn down an invitation to accompany him or her to the cinema and explain that you had other plans for that day. You might say that you did not like something that the other person had done or said. Are you wincing, saying to yourself: 'I could never do that!'? Try a small experiment first, not a major infringement of your rule, and see what happens.

The list of advantages and disadvantages of the belief 'I must be liked by everybody' was written by Ruth, a young nursing student. Ruth was so afraid of being disliked that she never said no to anything and she never showed any anger, even when people took advantage of her. An occasion presented itself when she could act against her personal rule. A friend arranged to meet her for a game of badminton and just did not turn up. The friend's only excuse was that she had not felt like it at the time and she had not even bothered to telephone to cancel the arrangements. Ruth was angry and normally she would have kept the anger to herself and made some mild, accepting comment. This time, she actually told her friend that she had felt angry, waiting for nothing and that she thought that the friend had been inconsiderate. To her surprise, the friend was in total agreement, apologised profusely and did not reject her. In fact, the friendship became stronger because both young women felt they could be more open and more straightforward with each other.

Anti-perfection tests are the easiest to set up. The prediction of the perfectionist is 'If I don't aim for 100%, I will become sloppy, I won't be respected, I won't be successful'. In fact, as you saw in the second example above, this attitude can interfere with your performance, with your degree of satisfaction and with your relationships. Try altering your standards and check the results. Take any of your activities and instead of aiming for 100%, aim for 80% or 60%. Then see how good your results are and how much enjoyment you get from the activities. You may find that the level of your performance increases, that the anxiety vanishes and you can interact more easily with your friends and colleagues.

The perfectionist attitude in the example given above was described by Peter, a university lecturer. Peter was getting into difficulty with his Head of Department, because of his poor productivity. Although he worked long hours, papers were never completed on time and he took three times as long as anybody else to mark students' work. He had also given up his favourite sport, squash, because he was making mistakes for which he could not forgive himself. He decided to run two experiments. He handed over the paper he had drafted, although he knew that it was not perfect. His Professor was very pleased and congratulated him on it. He made some minor corrections, but he did not think that Peter had been sloppy. With his squash, Peter decided to set up a game with his usual partner, with the aim of playing about 50% of the normal level he expected of himself. The result was that he enjoyed himself and won the game.

Richard who feared disapproval and ridicule from others tested his belief by deciding to reveal more about himself. He achieved this by doing things he had avoided at all costs before. Richard had never given a party before, in case the party was a flop and his friends would then think poorly of him. He never asked questions which might expose his ignorance of a subject. Above all, he was afraid of making a fool of himself. He gave his very first party and although some friends left early, others appeared to be enjoying themselves. He could compare his party to other parties he had attended and concluded that his was no worse on the whole. At work, in discussion with his colleagues, he asked a question because he did not fully understand the point that somebody was trying to make. He discovered that two other people did not understand either, that the person making the point was able to explain without making him feel a fool and without rejecting him.

Testing your basic rules can be difficult and may raise your anxiety as it involves doing what you have avoided doing before. However, if you start with easier tests, you will be encouraged by your results and your fear of breaking the rule will decrease gradually. You can think of it as a gradual retraining. If somebody is afraid of heights, say, the best way of overcoming the fear is by gradual exposure to increasing heights so that he or she can experience the situations without the predicted disasters.

Similarly, you will be more likely to relinquish or modify your rules, as you learn through experience that no disaster ensues if you break them.

12. How to Maintain Your Well-being

When your depression has improved, there are a few precautions you can take to help maintain your hard earned well-being. Depression is a very painful condition, as some of you might have experienced. Like a bad wound, it leaves a scar behind, even when you have defeated the depression. It takes a long time for the scar to heal completely. It is thought that this healing process may take at least six months, during which period there is the greatest risk of suffering a relapse.

If you have been treated with antidepressant medication, it is likely that your doctor will advise you to continue taking the medication for a further six months at least, although you may be completely recovered. If you have had many recurrences of depression in the past, the doctor may advise you to continue taking medication, antidepressants or lithium, for a much longer time.

If you have been treated with psychotherapy, maybe using the methods described in this book, your therapist will probably continue to see you at less frequent intervals for a further six months, to make sure that you are not having difficulties applying the techniques you learned during therapy.

Remember that often antidepressant drugs and therapy are used at the same time. Research has shown that there is no contraindication to using the two treatments in conjunction. In fact, the combined treatment is, often, more powerful than either treatment on its own.

In spite of, or perhaps because of, the suffering you have gone through with depression, you may find that you are a stronger person when you come out of the depression. You know yourself better and you are more aware of your assets and your liabilities. If you use the techniques that are described in this book, you can also make permanent changes which will be to your benefit. The advantage of

psychotherapy, and in particular of cognitive therapy, is that it enables you to learn techniques which you can then apply whenever you need to.

You have begun to learn new skills which you need to continue practising to increase your mastery, as you would do with any other skill. Let's say you learn to play the piano, maybe you did so as a child. If you discontinue practising at the keyboard, for any length of time, you soon forget what you have learned. The skills you have learned in this self-help manual to cope with depression are:

1. To combat inactivity by planning your work and increasing pleasant activities, so that you can improve

your mood by distraction and an increased sense of control.

2. To monitor your feelings and the thoughts which accompany them.

3. To write down your depressing thoughts and challenge and answer them, to get rid of the negative bias.

4. To increase your self-esteem and defeat guilt, hopelessness and indecision.

5. To become aware of your personal rules which may make you sensitive to certain types of situations.

6. To modify these rules by making them less global, less rigid and less demanding.

You can now continue practising these skills in your everyday life.

If you have been depressed in the past, you may be alarmed each time you experience low mood, wondering 'Am I getting depressed again?' Remember that it is normal for our mood to fluctuate. You will recognise the early signs of depression, as pointed out in Chapter 4, if the low mood persists for two weeks and you begin to develop other symptoms, for example, a change in your sleep pattern, loss of appetite, increasing loss of interest and pleasure in your usual activities, gloom and pessimistic thinking.

If this happens, go back to the section of the book you found most useful and start doing the exercises again. You will find that as your skill increases, you will be able to do most of the corrections mentally, without having to go through the process of writing down your thoughts. However, be careful not to be too hasty to reach this stage — it takes a lot of practice to get there.

You will also find it useful to go back to the written work you did before, so that you can rehearse the arguments you used before and perhaps add to them.

All this may sound like hard work, but it really is not. Thinking is something you do anyway and since more realistic thinking and problem-solving will help your well-being, it is worth it.

Good luck.

Useful Addresses

Cognitive Therapy
Your general practitioner can refer you to a cognitive therapist, usually a clinical psychologist or a psychiatrist, in your local health service.

Manic Depressive Fellowship
c/o Richmond-upon-Thames Council for Voluntary
Service
51 Sheen Road
Richmond
Surrey
Tel. 01-940-6235

Manic Depressive Fellowship
Scottish Association for Mental Health
40 Shandwick Place
Edinburgh   EH2 4RT
Tel. 031-225-4446

Depressives Anonymous
36 Chestnut Avenue
Beverley
N. Humberside HU17 9QU
Tel. 0482 860619

A self-help organisation for people with depression.
Co-ordinates self-help groups throughout the country.

Depressives Associated
PO Box 5
Castletown
Portland
Dorset   DT5 1BQ

Layman's help only to fellow-sufferers from depression.

Relaxation for Living.
29 Burwood Park Road
Walton-on-Thames
Surrey   KT11 5LH

Promotes the teaching of relaxation techniques to combat stress, strain, anxiety and tension.

Association for Post-Natal Illness
7 Gowan Avenue
Fulham
Richmond-Upon-Thames
London   SW6 6P4

Mama (Meet a Mum Association)
2 Railway Terrace
Pontrillas
Hereford HR2 0BH

Self-help group for women suffering from post-natal depression

Mind
National Association for Mental Health
22 Harley Street
London   W1N 2ED
Tel. 01-637-0741

Scottish Association for Mental Health
40 Shandwick Place
Edinburgh   EH2 4RT
Tel. 031-225-4446

Independent voluntary organisations concerned with all aspects of mental illness and mental health.

The Samaritans
54 Frederick Street
Edinburgh EH2 1LN
Tel. 031 225 3333
Or your local telephone directory for nearest branch.

Further Reading

The Diagnosis and Management of Depression

A T Beck
(University of Pennsylvania Press, Philadelphia, 1973)

Feeling Good. The New Mood Therapy

D D Burns
(William Morrow & Co Ltd, New York 1980)

Depression. What is It? How Do We Cope?

J Dominian
(Fontana Collings, 1970)

The Experience of Depression

D Rowe
(Wiley, New York & Chichester 1978)

Beating Depression

A J Rush
(Century Publishing Co Ltd, 1983)